"Ahh, women's orgasm… What do we typically read about it? It's that moment of climax and release that eludes so many women. Some women fake it, and some simply do without. Some women have multiple orgasms, they say. Autobiography of an Orgasm turns all of that on its head. This book is thoughtful, personal, poignant and surprising. It will give you a great many answers, but much more important, it will show you that you've been asking the wrong questions. Betsy's quest to "feel more" took her around the world, showed tremendous courage, and reaped rewards that went far beyond that fleeting moment that most of us think of as orgasm."
—Amanda, Phen Phnom, CAMBODIA

"Oh. My. Gosh. I swear you were writing about me. You spoke for me. You allowed me to see myself and appreciate myself in a way I never have. It was such an emotional read for me because I felt so connected to your story. Thank you. Absolutely amazing."
—Allison, Maryland, USA

"*Autobiography of an Orgasm* is one of those books you sit down and read in one sitting and every couple pages there is a line that changes everything and feels like a puzzle piece of your soul just got clicked back in. In the courageous dance so many of us take in healing past trauma and abuse and trying everything only to end up with the only thing that works back at the temple of our own body. Her exploration of orgasm as a spiritual awakening through spiritual embodiment is honest, erotic and a must read for all men who are inspired to hear the inner workings of a woman's journey and all women who want to breathe a sigh of relief that we finally live in a time and in a way that we can say our truth out loud and the truth will set us free."
—Rochelle Schieck, California, USA
Founder of Qoya www.loveqoya.com

"I would call it "when erotica meets how-to" as it's both entertaining and educational. Women will love it!"
—Hermoine, Athens, GREECE

"Through telling her own story she will sometimes make you laugh, and at other times seem to beg of you the question, are you living your truth? Are you authentically noticing and owning, each day, the beauty of living the soulful life that is your birthright? Do you experience meaning and intimacy as you interact with the world? And if not, when will you begin your personal journey to live a more simple, honest, divinely pleasurable life? I find it inspiring, downright delightful, to imagine the person that can heal, forgive, and thrive by identifying in some way with Betsy's reverently truthful and courageous autobiography of life up to this point."
—Jeannie, Indiana, USA

"This sexy-spiritual memoir ventures into delicate territory with so much honesty, courage, wit, and writing talent. It's a valuable story not simply for women on a quest to solve a problem but for any woman or man interested in the fullest sexual and spiritual experience."
—Peggy Payne, author of Cobalt Blue and other novels of sex and spirituality
www.peggypayne.com

# Autobiography

## of an **Orgasm**

Betsy Blankenbaker

*For Sara ♡*
*I hope this inspires*
*the story of your O.*
*love from Betsy*

# CONTENTS

For Sheri McKain who always helped me find humor in the moments where I only found sadness. I wish you had lived long enough to hear the rest of the story.

# INTRODUCTION

*"Vulnerability is the birthplace of connection and the path to the feeling of worthiness. If it doesn't feel vulnerable, the sharing is probably not constructive."*
—Brene Brown

This is a collection of stories about my five years of researching orgasm. I decided to research orgasm as a way to feel as much as possible after too many years of feeling nothing.

The journey led me to being in bed with orgasm experts, walking down Fifth Avenue in New York City with a 'healing' jade egg in my vagina, experiencing a spiritual awakening through orgasm in Africa, transporting a lover to the hospital with a fractured penis, volunteering to demo orgasm in front of forty people, honoring my womb near the Amazon in Peru, and finally returning to Indiana to finish this book. Indiana was the place where the early damage was done. I'd been running from it my whole life. But it was also the place I first started writing stories as a child, in a treehouse my dad built in the yard, away from the bedroom where I had been molested by a neighbor. That was the place I went to dream bigger dreams.

I started and stopped the book often during the past two years of writing (or not writing). I distracted myself with other projects and family emergencies until finally the discomfort of not telling the story was worse than the transparency of telling it.

# NOTE TO READERS:

This work is a memoir. It reflects the author's present recollection of her life. Certain names, including those of every man mentioned as a partner or lover, locations, and identifying characteristics have been changed. (One man did allow me to share our story using his name; maybe you can guess who he is in the book). Dialogue and events have been recreated from memory to convey the substance of what happened and they represent the author's recollection of the events. In some passages, the author has combined multiple incidents into one story to give the essence of what she experienced.

# ONE
## RUNNING AWAY

*"Shame is the most powerful, master emotion. It's the*
*fear that we're not good enough."*
—Brene Brown

I had my first orgasm when I was thirty-six, which means I spent half my life faking it. But really, the lies started much earlier. When I was young, I learned what to say and what to hide based on the feedback I got from people around me, like my parents, siblings, friends, coaches and teachers. Everyone responded differently, so I learned to put on a different mask and live a different truth, or a different lie, with each of them.

I had two homes growing up. I had my parents' house, where I lived with my four siblings, and I had my godparents' house, where I lived with Betty and Bill. When I was born in 1963, my parents already had three children, two girls and a boy, so with my birth, they weren't hoping for anything in particular. I was the result of an unplanned pregnancy.

False contractions sent my mom to the hospital three days before I was born. My dad, Richard, had been stocking the shelves of our family-run grocery store, Richard's Market Basket, when he got the call to come home and drive mom to the hospital. Several hours later, the contractions stopped, and my parents returned home. They were too tired to notice the red spots popping up on my oldest sister Susan. By the time I was born a few days later, my other sister Sharon and my brother David had the chicken pox as well.

My godparents offered to take me to their house and care for me until my siblings were better. It was an easy offer for my parents to accept since their backyard was just over the fence from ours. A few days after my birth, my mom went home with my dad, and I went home with Betty and Bill. Their teenage daughters, Wendy and Cathy, were waiting to greet me, excited to share their home with a baby. While my exhausted parents were home covering dozens of red spots on my siblings with calamine lotion, I can imagine myself gazing from my crib at my new "god family" and thinking, "*now this is more like it.*"

I stayed with my godparents for several weeks. My siblings had been free of chicken pox for over a week before my mom walked through the backyard gate to bring me home. As soon as I could crawl, I would head towards the gate to Betty's house. And then I walked there. My brothers and sisters rarely followed me; Betty's house was my place.

When I was three, my parents found a bigger home five miles away. In the weeks before the move, Betty taught me how to use the phone to call her. The rotary dial felt heavy under my small fingers, but I practiced, and I memorized the number. After we moved, Betty locked the gate to her backyard.

Moving into the bigger house meant I no longer had to share a bedroom with my brothers; I finally had my own room, and I loved it. My mom had covered one wall with scenes from my favorite book, *Snow White and the Seven Dwarfs*. I can still remember looking at that wallpaper while I was being molested by my neighbor. I was six.

It was a beautiful summer day when Val, a teenage neighbor, invited me to play. She said we needed to use one of our bedrooms. The four homes around us had families with lots of kids, so I guess it wasn't strange to my mom to see me come into the house with an older girl. Val was seven years older than me, closer to my oldest sister's age. I liked the attention from an older friend. She told me to lie down on my bed. We were going to play doctor.

"Take off your shorts. I need to check you."

I had never played doctor before, but I did as I was told. I pushed my shorts down to my knees.

"Take off your underwear too," she said.

I didn't know the rules. I pushed my underwear down, even though I remembered my godfather was a real doctor, and he never asked me to remove my underwear.

I felt a tickle as she glided her fingers across my belly. I had been in a swimming pool earlier in the day, and I watched her fingers leaving tracks on my dry skin.

"Open your legs," she said. I opened them as wide as my underwear and shorts around my knees would allow. She rubbed my thighs and then up to the place where pee came out of me. I didn't know what to call it. I felt butterflies in my belly when she touched me. It felt good. I didn't want to look at her, so I turned my head and looked at the wallpaper. Snow White was inches from my face, smiling at me.

Suddenly, it felt like she was tearing me apart. Her fingers were inside me. She put her other hand on my mouth. "Say nothing," she said. She didn't sound like my friend anymore. I held my breath and tightened my legs, hoping to squeeze her out of me.

I finally asked if we could switch, I would be the doctor. The minute she agreed, I pulled up my shorts and said I had to go to the bathroom. I ran downstairs and passed my mom in the kitchen. I was afraid I'd be in trouble if I spoke up, so I put on my first mask. I smiled and pretended that everything was okay. Behind the mask, I felt safe, like nothing bad had happened. Behind the mask, I knew my mom could still love me.

I went outside into the warmth of the summer afternoon where my brothers were riding bikes in our driveway, as if everything was fine. I went around to the side of the house and lay in the grass at the top of a small hill, trying to be invisible. My heart was beating so fast I thought it might pop through my shirt. I looked at the sky and remembered a game I loved playing where I used my mind to break up the clouds. If I focused hard enough on a cloud, I could make it disappear. It always worked.

I stayed there until the sun disappeared. That night I called my godparents to come pick me up. After my godmother prepared my bath, I took off my underwear. There were dots of blood on it like when I had a bloody nose. When Betty wasn't looking, I rolled the panties in toilet paper and hid them in the trash.

The room I slept in at my godparents' house was pale blue like a robin's egg. There was a framed picture above my bed with the words from "A Prayer For Children". My godmother and I said the prayer when I slept over. The words meant nothing to me until that night when I said, "And if I die before I wake, I pray to God my soul to take."

"I don't want to die tonight," I said to Betty.

"You won't," she smiled. "I promise."

"Then why do we say that prayer?"

"It's a prayer to God to guide us to be good during our days and to let us rest at night."

She kissed me good night and shut the door. I kept my eyes open as long as possible, worried that God would enter the room to take my soul if I fell asleep because of what had happened that day. How do you live without a soul?

I never spoke up about the neighbor hurting me. I didn't know how to talk about those things, so I kept it a secret, even at Betty's house. And then it happened again a few years later. I was walking home from piano lessons, and some boys in the neighborhood came upon me very quickly. They pushed me into the bushes and grabbed at the crotch of my pants. As I moved my hands to shield myself, they grabbed at my chest. We played this game, with me moving my hands to protect my body and them moving their hands to the exposed areas. I was no match for six hands. Finally, a car drove by, honked, and the boys ran off, laughing. When I got home I tried to scrub the grass stains out of my pants. The next week when it was time to walk to my piano lesson, I told my mom I wanted to quit. She said she was disappointed in me, but I still refused to go. It was easier to put on a mask that carried her disappointment than to tell her the truth about being violated. I was afraid I had done something wrong. I was worried she wouldn't love me.

# BETSY BLANKENBAKER

*"In every conceivable manner, the family is link to our past, bridge to our future."*
—Alex Haley

When I was little, I wanted to be like my older sisters, Susan and Sharon, even though I had short hair, and people confused me for a boy. My sisters were taking dance lessons, so I took them too. I pinned all the pieces of my short hair into the tiniest bun so I looked like a ballerina. I held my shoulders back and pointed my toes when I walked. I practiced jumping and twirling in the huge family room in our house, in my own version of a ballerina who also liked to shake and shimmy. I was a ballerina until the day I overheard the Russian ballet instructor telling my mom that I was not as good as my sisters. After stopping the lessons, I danced only in my room. It felt sneaky to still dance after hearing I was no good. After ballet, I moved on to swimming.

When I joined the swim team, I discovered my body enjoyed being in the pool. Before practice, we undressed in the locker rooms and stored our clothes in wire baskets during practice. I undressed and quickly pulled on my swimsuit. I didn't want to be naked or see anyone else naked.

One morning when I was twelve, I woke up with sticky, brownish-red stains on my underwear. I knew it was my period, but I didn't know what it meant. Period was the term mentioned by girls on the swim team for the bleeding they occasionally experienced. I wasn't too sure where it was coming from or what it meant. Some of the girls would skip practice during their period. Some of the girls still swam. It was all very confusing to me.

When I felt the warm blood in my panties that morning, I knew where to go – straight to my older sister Susan's bathroom. Susan was seven years older than I and had a cabinet full of lotions and potions. When she wasn't home, I would go into her bathroom and look through the shelves, curious what all the bottles were used for.

On the day of my first period, I went into Susan's bathroom and locked the door. Suddenly, I heard my dad shouting. He announced we were leaving for church in ten minutes. It was Sunday! My mom had left earlier with my sisters. I wasn't comfortable asking them for help anyway. We never talked about our bodies.

I took off my panties and put them in the sink to soak the stains in warm water as I looked for the box filled with tampons. I tore the paper off one and held the plastic tube. I looked in the box and found a folded paper inside. I unfolded the paper; it was a large sheet with instructions in both English and French. Knowing there was not time enough, I skipped the reading and studied the illustrations instead. The slender fingers in the drawings showed how to angle the tampon up into the vagina. It was a word we didn't use in my family. I was twelve, and my vagina had been nameless.

My dad knocked on the door. I jumped.

"Almost ready, Bets?"

"Yes! Be down in a minute."

I sat on the lid of the toilet with my feet braced against the cool marble of the bathtub. I looked away, out the tiny window in the bathroom, as I barely opened my legs and tried to stick the tampon inside me. I had never touched myself down there. I gently poked the head of the tampon into the direction of my vagina, but it wouldn't slide inside me. I looked at the instructions again. *Relax the vaginal wall,* it advised. I had no idea how to do that. I took a deep breath and closed my eyes and rubbed the tip of the tampon slowly along my vaginal area until I could feel an opening.

"We're getting in the car," Dad yelled. "Let's go." I could see my dad and brothers out the window.

I'm on my way to church, I thought. If there is a God, please help me get this inside me.

I pushed again and felt some discomfort. I looked down and saw most of the tampon had disappeared in me, but I could still feel some of it hanging out of me. Even though it was uncomfortable, I decided that to push again might make it worse. I slid the plastic tube covering the tampon out of me and quickly pulled on tights and a skirt. I walked out to the car feeling the tampon wedged between my legs, wondering if anyone would notice.

After that when I got my period, I imagined my vagina looked like the colorless black and white illustration on the tampon instructions. When I inserted the tampon, I always looked away, never curious to see what I really looked like.

In middle school and high school, many of my friends made out with the boys, and some were even having sex. I kissed a few boys, but I didn't want them touching my body. Every muscle would tighten when a boy tried to do more than kiss me. My body felt most comfortable covered unless I was at swim practice; there I would relax into the rhythm of my strokes doing lap after lap. I was a fast swimmer, and I felt safe in the pool.

And then one day, even the pool wasn't safe for me. I was sixteen and training at the Indianapolis Athletic Club. The IAC was established in the 1920s to promote "clean sports, amusement and sociability" for its members. When I was training at the IAC in 1979, women members of the club still didn't have voting rights. The club had accepted its first African- American members a few years earlier, but usually the only African-Americans you would see were working there. I trained there because of the excellent swim coach.

The swimming pool was on the lower level of the club. The elevator had an attendant dressed in a black suit with white gloves. Every day before practice, I entered the elevator on the main floor and rode two levels down. I smelled chlorine before the doors opened. I always greeted the elevator attendant, an older man, even though I thought it was silly to pay someone to press the buttons. I never told him which floor. He always knew where I needed to go.

But one day, the minute he pressed the LL button for Lower Level, he turned and pushed himself against me, grabbing at my shirt and pants. There were mirrors on the walls of the elevator and I could see images of

7

his white gloves attacking my body from all angles. I tucked my head down as he tried to push his warm tongue in my mouth. I was strong from swimming, but not strong enough to push him away. My voice left me. It was a relief to smell the chlorine and to know we were almost to the pool. And then just as quickly as he'd started, he stopped, and the doors opened.

"Don't tell anyone," he warned before the doors shut. "Or you'll get in trouble."

I said hello to my coach and dove into the water so I didn't have to talk to anyone else. Another mask. The next week I quit swimming.

The following year I graduated from high school a year early. I was seventeen years old when I left for college in Dallas, Texas. Going away meant leaving the wounds and memories of Indiana behind. I didn't realize all the masks I was carrying with me.

The first time I made the choice to allow a man inside me, I was eighteen. It was the end of my freshman year in college. Even with consent, it was not much better than my previous experiences. It was hard to breathe beneath his heavy body. He was not gentle. None of it felt good. I didn't say a word.

"You're on your period?" he asked when he saw blood on his sheets.

I shook my head no and wrapped the sheet around me as I walked into the bathroom. I stuck the sheet in his sink and ran warm water. I scrubbed until any sign of me was gone.

Sophomore year I started dating Oliver, a golfer from Arizona. He was a year older than me.

I wanted a redo on losing my virginity, so I told him I was a virgin. He was the first man to tell me he loved me, so I loved him back. I was still fumbling through sex, always letting him show me the way. Six months into dating him, even though I was on the pill, I missed my period. My having an abortion was the only option we discussed. He left money in the top drawer of my dresser and left town for a golf tournament. I found the name of a clinic near Plano, a thirty-minute drive from campus. It seemed far enough from Dallas. I took the money he gave me and drove myself to the clinic.

"You have someone to drive you home after the procedure?" the nurse asked as she poked my arm for a vein. I nodded, even though I didn't. My ride was three hours away playing a tournament in Austin, and I'd been too ashamed to tell anyone else I was a few weeks pregnant. I felt a wave of relief pass through my body as the nurse injected me with painkiller. The medicine flowing through my veins made me feel good enough not to care about what was happening next.

My legs were spread.

A man I'd never met, the doctor, sat between my thighs.

"You're going to feel a tug," he said.

I could hear the suck of the vacuum.

I looked at his expressionless eyes and wanted to yell "stop!", but the drugs made my tongue heavy.

After the procedure, I sat in a recovery area with five other women. None of us spoke to each other. I wondered where the tiny pieces of our six embryos ended up as we sat together in silence. I don't think any of us felt whole anymore.

When it was time to leave, my panties were packed with pads. I was given ice packs and pain medicine. I told them my fiancé was pulling up the car. I left the clinic groggy, but I came to life when I heard the protestors outside. I quickly got into my car, locked the door and put the ice pack between my legs. My vagina and abdomen were throbbing. I slowly pulled my car out of the clinic parking lot as a group of protestors about my parents' age screamed "baby killer!" at me and thrust their placards up, blocking my view. Did they think their words were any worse than what I was already screaming to myself?

I drove home and stayed in bed for two days. I told my roommate I was sick. The third day, I met friends for lunch. It was my nineteenth birthday.

The following year, I told a few friends about my abortion, but mainly I ignored the damage and shame I felt by choosing to end a pregnancy. Maybe the memory would go away just like the other things I didn't want to talk about. The mask I put on that day was heavy. It was the ugliest one I could find.

I married twice in my twenties. The first time was to the first man to ask me. I resented my godmother Betty when she said she didn't think I should marry him. Her objection wasn't about him – she didn't think I was ready. She was right; I was married less than two years. When I said yes to the next man who asked me to marry him, my godmother thought I was ready that time. So did I. Once again, my friends and family gathered for another wedding for me. This one just three years after the first one. I was rushing ahead with life, or maybe I was running away. I put on another wedding dress and said "I do."

Ben and I were together for ten years. We were either giving birth to children or renovating homes the entire time we were married. We created a lot in ten years: Four children and six homes, and that didn't count our jobs. Ben was a music producer. I worked in film and video production, but I quit working when I got pregnant with our first child.

The first time I met Ben, he left me a message later that day on my answering machine that he was going to marry me. Our first date lasted seven hours. We talked and talked through an early happy hour and then a late dinner. After dinner, as we walked to our cars, a couple passed by us. The woman looked at us and said, "It's good to see people so in love."

"We just met," I said laughing.

"You should marry her," the woman said looking at Ben.

The next month, Ben surprised me with a puppy, but said he was keeping the dog at his house. It was a great way to seduce me to stay with him. We named the dog Jack. We married a year later.

Ben was a passionate lover, and I was grateful for his large, strong cock. It was the most beautiful cock I had ever seen. He was slow and thoughtful when he made love to me. Even though he was distracted with work during the day, he kept all his attention on me when we had sex. We also had fun in bed. He made me laugh, and it was nice to bring that playfulness into the bedroom. When we finished, he would keep his arm around me until we fell asleep, as Jack slept at the foot of our bed. I loved feeling the heat of his body next to me if I woke up during the night. For the first time, sex was starting to feel safe and comfortable for me, but I still lied about my orgasm.

I told him about the shame around my abortion. He didn't judge me. I never told him about the early abuse or about not feeling safe in my body. I never told him I felt damaged or that I didn't allow myself to feel my orgasm. Too many painful things had happened to my vagina, and they left me believing that I didn't deserve to feel good. I didn't deserve to have an orgasm. It never occurred to me that my movements in bed might reveal me. Or that every time I faked an orgasm, I was adding more damage to my womb instead of healing it. Speaking the truth didn't feel like an option, so I pretended everything was okay.

Ben was an atheist, but when we made love one afternoon in April, he looked me in the eyes as he was cuming in me and said, "I pray to God that I just got you pregnant." I had our first baby nine months later.

I don't remember how the tradition started, but every day I would ask Ben what was his favorite thing about me.

"Your smile," he said.

The next day he would answer "your legs" or "watching you breastfeed" or "how sexy you look when you are driving the kids in the Suburban."

It was our ritual, our tradition in a marriage that kept getting lost in building a larger home, in taking on more friends and more job responsibilities, and in spending less time together. By my fourth pregnancy, he had the #1 hit in the country, but it seemed like the bigger his career grew, the smaller our marriage became.

One day Ben came home from the studio not looking happy. I thought I could beguile him into feeling good again. I came up behind him and put my arms around his waist and asked, "What's your favorite thing about me today?"

"Why do you always ask me that?" he said. I could feel him pulling away. Or maybe it was me. I never asked him that question again.

The joy we experienced in creating a family was matched by great loss in our own lives. Ben's father died. I lost my father, godfather and godmother. My best friend got ovarian cancer. And then I lost my fifth child, a baby boy I delivered at twenty weeks. It took the baby dying for me to realize my marriage was dead, too.

Ben and I fixed so many homes, but we never tried repair our marriage. There were so many losses, I wasn't even sure what the problem was until one day a year later, a letter arrived in the mail.

The long white business envelope was addressed to my husband. I stared at the envelope; the handwriting looked familiar, but I couldn't place it. I put the letter with the rest of the mail on the desk Ben and I shared. We were still living together as we worked through the details of a divorce. Our four children were under the age of eight, and we both wanted to hold on to our family as we let go of each other.

I looked at the stack of mail again and picked up the white envelope. Whoever wrote the address was not in a rush; every letter looked perfectly formed. I turned the envelope over. No return address. I glanced at the clock knowing he would be home soon, and then I slowly slid my finger along the seal of the envelope and pulled out a thick bundle of white paper. At the top of the first page in large handwritten letters it said, Read & Burn. *Dear Ben*, it began.

I read through the five pages without taking a full breath. The writer was in pain after being dismissed by my husband, *MY Dear Ben,* whom she called a lover and a best friend. She detailed their sex life while describing my inadequacy in the bedroom. She said I had a "lack of zeal", and she reminded him how much she had pleased him. She called herself his fuck buddy and wondered how he could walk away from her. She said she was the best thing to ever happen to him. As I read the last line of the letter, I recognized the handwriting as Lea's. She was my best friend. I had dinner plans with her that night, and as I dialed her number to cancel, I prayed to get her answering machine. She picked up.

"Hello."

I felt numb when I heard her voice.

"Hi, it's Betsy," I said. "I can't do to dinner tonight."

"Ok, how about tomorrow night?" she responded.

"I'm not sure. I'll call later and let you know," I said, knowing I never planned on speaking to her again. I hung up the phone without mentioning the letter. For me, it was easier to pretend everything was okay.

Ben and I divorced a year later, but not because of Lea. I had also cheated during the marriage, and the shame of cheating added to the pile of disapproval I felt about myself.

Ten years later, I found the letter mixed in with artwork and pictures from my children's childhood. I set it aside, thinking I might destroy it or pass it to Ben. I had no desire to bring up something from the past. Life was mostly good for us post-divorce. We still shared holidays and many dinners with the kids together. People said they admired us for making divorce look good because we got along so well. I never blamed Ben for wanting to be with someone else.

But something made me read the letter again.

Betsy's lack of sexual zeal, she wrote. I'm your fuck buddy.

Everything she wrote – the attacks on my sensuality, my lack of interest in sex – was true.

I was not a sensual being.

My vagina was a place of shame.

My vagina was a place of death.

I had never let my vagina feel pleasure.

I put down the letter. This time, instead of feeling sorry for myself and running away from everything, including my orgasm, I decided to to see if I could discover what it meant to be born into the body of a woman. I wanted to find out how to feel my orgasm and, maybe, how to feel my life, because at that point I wasn't feeling anything.

# TWO
## SEARCHING FOR MY O

*"Many, many of us have left our bodies — we're not
embodied creatures, we're not living inside our own
muscles and cells and sinews. And so we're not in our
power, we're not in our energy."*
—Eve Ensler

"How's your pussy?" screamed the voice coming from the woman dancing onto the stage. The voice belonged to Regena Thomashauer, founder
of the School of Womanly Arts (SWA), based in New York City. Most of
the two hundred women in the room jumped to their feet and danced
along with her. They all seemed happy and turned-on. I didn't get up to
dance; I stayed in my seat questioning my decision to sign up for the
course. I did not fit in.

I was 45 when I took the course with Regena. I'd been divorced for
almost ten years. At the time, there wasn't one specific problem – my life
just wasn't feeling good. The SWA course included experts in health,
wellness, diet, money, career, men, communication, sex and sensuality.
Maybe somewhere in all those lectures, I would find the answer. I was at a
point in my life where I was giving up, and the course seemed like the
most radical form of therapy I could do at the time.

Regena spoke with reverence for "pussy", her chosen word for vagina. It seemed like she was comparing it to the soul, something I'd never
thought much about, either. She was making the point that if you were
disconnected from your pussy, your feminine essence, you were disconnected from your soul.

Everything in class was "your pussy" this and "your pussy" that. I was uncomfortable hearing her use a word I considered vulgar to refer to a woman's genitals. I'd never had a name for my vagina, because I never spoke about it.

When Regena asked the class who had seen their pussies – again, her word choice, not mine – about half of the class raised their hands. I kept my hand down, and I was relieved to see I was not the only one. Maybe I did fit in.

The class included a slide show displaying photos of different vulvas and examples of art featuring women's genitals, such as the famous painting *L'Origin Du Monde,* painted by French artist Gustave Courbet in 1866. It was a close-up view of the genitals of a naked woman, lying on a bed with her legs spread. I had never seen another women's genitals close-up, and now I was looking at photo after photo after photo of vulvas on a huge screen. It was a lot of pussy to take in. Most of the images made me uncomfortable, but at the end of the class, I was curious to see mine.

That night I went back to my hotel room and used the make-up mirror in the bathroom to have a look. I lay on the floor and held the mirror between my legs. I took a quick glance. I could only see the outer lips of my vulva, much like the painting, *L'Origin du Monde*. I looked again and noticed the roundness where my ass met my thigh. I liked the reflection. I changed positions and sat on the edge of a chair. I put the mirror on the floor and tilted it up. Then I reached between my legs and pulled open the outer lips of my vulva. The outer edges of my vulva were a dark burgundy, but inside was a pretty shade of pink. The skin was moist and glistened in the dim bedroom lighting. I felt partly nauseated and partly thrilled, like when you're on a roller coaster and want to get off and keep going at the same time.

My vagina felt like silk as I ran my finger to the hood of my clit. I saw the tip of my clit pushing through. I was surprised how easy it was to find. I lightly touched it, and a contraction pulsed through my genitals and deep into my belly. When I pulled my hands away, the outer lips came together like drapes that were being pulled shut. The top of the lips formed a hood over my clit. The way the lips hung open reminded me of a statue of the Virgin Mary.

The next day, I sat near the back of the room when Steve Bodansky spoke to our class about orgasm. Steve and his wife Vera had written many books on the subject, and they were considered experts in extended massive orgasm, a term I'd never heard. Steve told of the turn-on he experienced bringing Vera, his long-term partner, to orgasm for over an hour, just by stroking her clitoris. They had also done demos where Vera would orgasm for over three hours. Vera was now in her 70s and was glowing. I was intrigued. As he spoke, I remembered the only time I allowed myself to feel my orgasm. It was with the man I had an affair with towards the end of my marriage and went on to date after my divorce.

I was 36 years old, and we had spent the day on the beach. My lover and I went back to our room for a nap, and as we fell asleep, he pulled his naked body, still warm from the sun and smelling of coconut oil, around mine like he was wrapping me in a blanket. I woke up from the nap with tingling in my body. His lips and hands were between my legs. His tongue was softly licking my clit. His fingers circled the lips of my vulva.

My first instinct was to stop him, to switch positions and go down on him. My body wanted to please, not to be pleased. He moved a hand to each of my thighs to hold me in place, and the pressure made my legs open further. I reached down and ran a finger through a dark curl on his head, slightly stiff from the salt water. I wanted to guide him to my mouth to kiss me, but instead he moved his lips to taste me. A wave of wetness flooded into my vagina as I let out a soft sigh.

His fingers grasped my thighs and his thumbs met at my vulva. He used his thumbs to rub just inside my vagina as his tongue played with my clit, each slow lick taking me deeper into ecstasy. He alternated between exploring my clit with his tongue, then his finger, and then blowing on it while his thumbs explored the opening of my vagina. It felt like 1,000 lights were being turned on inside me, each lick or touch turning on another switch. My breath slowed, and with each inhalation, I felt the light that was pulsing through my vagina rise into the rest of my body.

The feeling of pleasure made me uncomfortable. I wanted to wiggle out of his arms and disconnect from the explosion of energy. He gently held on, keeping me in place so I could only receive. I inhaled deeply, and my shoulders softened as the muscles in my legs relaxed. My body melted into the bed and into his mouth and into his hands. Even the softest brush of his lips along my vulva sent shocks of energy deep into my core. But while the inside of me buzzed like fireworks being lit, my throat was constricting. I wanted to cry, scream and rage at everyone from my past – especially myself – who didn't treat my body as sacred.

I took a hard breath, and from the darkness in my throat, words finally came.

"Thank you, thank you, thank you," I whispered.

Tears dripped down my cheeks as I watched the late afternoon sun fade from the room. Afterwards, lying in my lover's arms, my entire body still throbbed. As we fell back to sleep, I was too ashamed to tell him it was my first time to feel my orgasm.

The next time I came was with a vibrator. My lover lived in a different state, and we only saw each other every few months, so I got used to using a vibrator to climax. I became an expert at getting myself off within minutes. What I didn't do was share my use of this new toy with my lover. There were some things I was not ready to talk about. He was an amazing, tender lover and a good friend, but I never allowed myself to climax again with him. Deep down, I associated feeling good with those first sensations I enjoyed before I was assaulted when I was six. To avoid that memory, I went back to faking it with him like I did with everyone else.

My lover supported me through the production and release of my first film, which I produced as my marriage was ending. It was a documentary based on the book by Dan Wakefield, *New York in the Fifties*, about the young writers, musicians and artists living in Greenwich Village in the 1950s. The group arrived in NYC in their early twenties with hopes and dreams about their future. I interviewed Robert Redford, who lived as a young painter in NYC during that decade, and he said, "At the time, everything felt like it was on the verge of suicide, and that felt right, you know." In most cases, the artists' dreams shattered, and they picked up the pieces and started over again. It felt like my life after marriage, except I was not good at putting the pieces back together.

Two years after my divorce was settled, I met my lover for a weekend in New York City. His mother had died a few months earlier, and I had travelled with him back to France, where he and his siblings buried her. I loved him and his family deeply, but I was still living in a world of shame. I didn't feel worthy of a man who loved me so much. I know I didn't feel worthy of my own love. We were on the verge of breaking up before his mom died, so it surprised me when he proposed marriage during our weekend in New York. I said no, and my heart broke into a million pieces.

After we broke up, I continued to bring myself to climax with a vibrator, but the more I used a vibrator to get off, the smaller my orgasm was feeling. The climax with my lover had been brought on by the softest strokes, and the bliss exploded through my entire body for over an hour. By the time I heard Steve Bodansky speak about orgasm in 2008, my climax was small and quick. I needed more and more stimulation to feel less and less. I was pretty sure my use of a vibrator had desensitized my clit. Another woman in the audience was courageous enough to ask the question: "Can overusing a vibrator affect your climax?"

"Yes, the clit can be desensitized by a vibrator, making it harder to have an orgasm," said Steve.

"And if you do get off, the body may feel less of your orgasm," said Regena.

The woman looked disappointed.

My stomach sank, knowing Regena was speaking my truth.

"Why don't you try giving up a vibrator for a month? Research what it feels like to lightly stroke your clit for thirty days, for fifteen minutes a day," said Regena. "Your only goal is to feel each stroke, not to get off."

The woman agreed. I silently committed to the research, too.

Giving up my vibrator meant giving up the daily fix I was getting, where I would put the vibrator on high and firmly press it against my clit until I had a climax that lasted as long as a hiccup. I was powering my way through my orgasms. I was addicted to the climax.

I wasn't convinced that Regena's suggestion would work for my body, but I committed to the thirty days of stroking.

In the first days of my research, it was a relief to have the fifteen minute limit and to have dispensed with the goal, because for the first five days, I didn't feel a thing.

I stroked my clit with the lightest of strokes.

Nothing.

When I tried harder strokes, it was painful, like sandpaper being pulled over my clit.

I went back to the lighter strokes.

The second week I was inspired by a suggestion Regena gave in class, so I started speaking words of gratitude as I stroked.

I said things I'd never said before, and they didn't seem altogether true when I spoke them.

"Thank you for the gift of my body."

"Thank you for being a portal to bring my children into the world."

"Thank you for giving me the courage to research orgasm."

"Thank you for the gift of being a woman."

"Thank you for this single stroke."

"Thank you for my vagina."

While I wasn't feeling any sensation, the simplicity of the single stroke, slowly, over and over again, took me deeper into a meditative state each day. When my mind floated out of the stillness, I wondered if I was going crazy. Sometimes, I would cry.

I judged myself.

I voiced gratitude.

I hated myself.

I spoke of gratitude.

I let the tears flow.

For the first time, what I didn't do was fake it. I let myself stroke and express gratitude and feel nothing.

And then, on Day Eight, I felt something.

A flutter in my vagina.

She was remembering.

Every day after, the sensation expanded. By the thirtieth day, the tingling started with the first stroke and took my whole body and mind on a ride for the entire fifteen minutes.

I realized I was coming back home into the body I'd abandoned when I was six.

Thank you.

# THREE
## CONNECTING TO THE DIVINE

*"Your task is not to seek for love, but merely to seek*
*and find all the barriers within yourself that you have*
*built against it."*
—Rumi

For fun, I once had a woman read my palm. She gazed at my hand for several minutes, tracing the lines with her finger. She told me how many children I would have ("five, but one is different," she said) and how many men I would marry ("three"). I rolled my eyes thinking she's not so good. I'd been married twice in my twenties and didn't plan on another wedding. And, at first, I thought she was wrong about the children, I only had four. And then I remembered my fifth baby died, maybe that was what she meant by one was different.

She said I'd have a long life. Then she stopped and looked closer at a line on my palm. "Have you had your near death experience yet?"

I looked down at my hand to try and see what she was seeing.

"Ummm, no," I said.

"You will," she said confidently. "Don't worry, you won't die, but it will be the start of a shift in your life."

Four years later, I was in Florida meeting friends for a drink on their boat. My sandals were off, and as I walked through the grass to board the boat, I felt a sting. The electric shock went all the way up my leg. I didn't think much about it as I joined my friends onboard for a glass of champagne. Just as we toasted, a wave of heat flushed through my body. Sweat started pouring from my face, arms and legs.

"I think I'm going to be sick," I said to my friend, Kris.

I could tell from her face that I didn't look good.

"Let me take you inside to the bathroom," she said.

I felt dizzy as I stood up. Kris took my arm to steady me, and we walked the few feet to the cabin of the boat. My heart was racing and pounding like it would break through my chest. My throat was constricting; I couldn't get a breath. I started to get scared when I felt like I was suffocating. I heard Kris's voice yell for help as I hit the floor.

And then it was peaceful. I was floating in white space. I was connected to everything around me, like my body didn't end, it expanded past the skin. All the painful sensations were gone. I could breathe. I wasn't afraid anymore.

I heard voices. They didn't belong to any of my friends, but they sounded like regular voices, as if suddenly there were more people on the boat with us.

"She's not supposed to be here yet," I heard. "She has to go back."

I was content staying right where I was, floating in a space that reminded me of the peace I felt as a child when I lay in the grass and looked at the clouds, connecting to the sky and the earth at the same time. I felt that peace holding my newborn baby, watching a sunset or being surprised by a rainbow. I felt that peace when a favorite song came on the radio or when I was dancing. I felt that peace when I fell in love. In those moments, there was a knowingness, a confirmation, of the deeper truths that can only be felt, not learned.

More discussion swirled around me, but none of the the voices were talking to me.

I don't know where I am, I thought, but I don't want to leave. My entire being surrendered to whatever would happen next. Both outside and inside my body felt balanced and whole; there was no split or struggle to hide parts of me.

I wanted to ask if I could stay. I turned my head toward the voices to speak. They ignored me. It seemed like they knew what was on my mind: Don't make me go back. It feels so good here.

"She can't stay. She's still supposed to…"

And with those words, I suddenly saw Kris and my other friends' faces above me. I was back in my body, lying on the floor and looking up at them. My clothes were drenched with sweat. My breathing was back to normal. Kris helped me sit up and got me a class of water. I was too dazed to tell her what I saw on the other side. A friend took me to the ER and they checked my vitals. The doctor said I had gone into anaphylactic shock from being bitten by a bug.

"You're lucky to be alive," he said.

I didn't tell him that part of me wanted to stay on the other side, where my body, mind and soul were free from the heaviness I chose to carry with me in life. I didn't tell the doctor that by coming back to life, I didn't feel so lucky.

*"This sky where we live is no place to lose your wings.*
*So love, love, love."*
—Hafiz

I was not on a spiritual path before I began my orgasm research, but the voices I heard during my near death experience made me think there may be a higher power or connection I had never considered. I rejected God because of the dogma I grew up with in the church. God was separate, judgmental (Thou Shalt Not!), and God didn't seem to be present when I needed him. And if there was a God, I questioned if God was only a Him. The four major religions, Christianity, Judaism, Islam and Hinduism had no women in leadership positions. Even the spiritual knowledge of Buddhism was led by men. As a woman, how did that kind of God fit into my life?

As I started my research, I began to think about the possibility of a God within each of us. I recognized that if God is love, and God is within me, then God and love have *always* been present in my life. It made me see the scene in my childhood bedroom in a completely different way, knowing that my love was still present even when something bad was happening to me. The only person withholding love all these years had been me.

About five years before I started my research on orgasm, there was one man in my life who brought a sacred essence into our lovemaking and opened me to consider a more spiritual path. Oddly, it was an accident during sex that brought me closer to a connection with God/the Source/Divinity when we made love.

His name was Eli. He worked on a private yacht in the Caribbean and Bahamas. I was living in Miami with my four small children. We saw each other every few weeks when he was in port. Usually, he came to Miami and stayed with my family, but one weekend my children were visiting their dad, so I got on a plane and flew to the Bahamas to meet him.

Eli was ten years younger than I, but in many ways his was the older soul. The year before I met him, he was a successful stockbroker living in the Midwest. At the time, he had a house, a BMW, a girl, and all the material things you dream of having when you are in your late twenties. Many of his close friends were getting married and having children. He was happy, but he decided to dream a bigger dream and give himself a few years of travel before he committed to the path most of his friends and family were choosing. He quit his job and sold his house, furniture and car. He left the Midwest where he'd lived all his life and took the job on the yacht. I met him when some good friends chartered it and invited me along as a guest.

One night after everyone else went to bed, I couldn't sleep, so I wandered up past the main and second decks where we suntanned during the day and took the small set of steps to the yacht's uppermost deck. I was surprised to see that Eli was there, too. I started to turn around, but he saw me first, so I joined him on the sofa, keeping my distance, as I did with everyone else.

It turned out we were both from the same city in Indiana, so we talked about why we'd left. As the boat cruised the peaceful waters of the Bahamas, we talked through the night, our conversation lit by the moon. I asked him how his year of travel was going. He asked me about my kids. I asked him what his favorite part of his job was. He asked me if he could kiss me.

His skin was golden from working in the sun, and his shaggy hair hung in his eyes. He looked like the actor Owen Wilson. I'd come on this trip to relax, not to get laid, but I said yes to the kiss, and that led to sex, but it was a slow, soft version of sex that matched the calmness of the water all around us. As he moved in and out of me, I peeked out from under my eyelids and saw his blue eyes gazing at me. I was uncomfortable staring back, so I looked away and up into the thousands of stars above me. Then I closed my eyes again and enjoyed the ride.

We started dating right away. We didn't see each other often, but when we did have time together, we spent most of it in bed. The pace of our dating was just right for me. I could let him into my life, but not too much. He was out of cell range most of the time he was working, so our communication was limited.

During our fourth month of dating, I flew to the Bahamas to see Eli when his boat was in port for the weekend. He picked me up at the airport, and we took a taxi across the island to a funky boutique hotel on the edge of the ocean. We sat outside and had a drink at the bar as the butterscotch sun started melting into the water. We didn't make it through the entire sunset. Eli took my hand and led me to the room.

The windows of our room were wide open. I felt a warm breeze on my body as Eli undressed me. We danced to the reggae band playing next door as we made our way to bed. I stood naked in front of him, swaying my hips. Some of my insecurities about my body had dissolved in the few months of dating him because he treated my body with appreciation and respect. It reminded me to do the same.

He took his shirt off and lay on the bed. I lowered myself on top of him and my lips followed the trail of his chest hair downward until it disappeared into his shorts. I pulled his shorts off his hips to reveal his gorgeous hard cock. That night it was larger and harder than I remembered. Usually we took time with foreplay, but after two weeks apart, he pulled me on top of him and slid inside me. I was already very wet. I stretched my arms towards the ceiling and let out a moan as my body opened to take him in. He lifted his hips to pulse in and out of me. I leaned forward and kissed him as his movements became faster. The reggae music grew louder. I felt the strength of his cock inside me. Each time he pumped more, my body floated a little higher and I came down harder as he thrust himself deeper inside me. I pulled my body upright, so I was rising and hovering just above his cock, and then I lowered myself down on top of him. It felt like freedom for my body to receive him so fully. He put his hands around my waist and guided me with each movement. We locked eyes, and this time I didn't look away.

Suddenly I heard a crack. He pushed me off him and ran to the bathroom. I heard him throwing up.

"You okay?" I said.

"Something's wrong," he said. As he walked towards me, I saw that his cock had shrunk, but his testicles were the size of a grapefruit. A little blood dripped from the head of his penis. Now I wanted to throw up.

He sat on the bed, doubled over in pain. I wasn't sure what was wrong. As a mother, I am good at taking care of first aid emergencies, but I had no idea what to do next.

I wrapped a sarong around me and ran to the bar for some ice. By the time I returned, his testicles had grown to the size of a cantaloupe. This can't be good, I thought.

"The bartender said there's a hospital about forty minutes away," I said. The color had drained from Eli's face.

"Bahamian hospitals are not great," he said. "Can you get my phone and call the boat? They can call a good doctor."

I pressed the captain's number and passed the phone to Eli. As he explained what happened, I could hear the captain laughing through the connection. It was certainly an unusual call to get during happy hour on a Friday evening. The captain was drinking with the rest of the boat's crew, and the laughter got louder as the information was relayed.

"Hold on, let me call the global medical assistance on the other line," said the captain.

I wrapped the ice in a towel and put it on Eli's groin while we waited. It was looking worse. His swollen balls were a deep burgundy shade. His penis wilted.

"I've got a doctor on the other line," said the captain. "He said if you heard a crack, then you need to go to the hospital." He was still laughing as he relayed the info. "Did you hear a crack?"

We both nodded our heads.

"Yes," said Eli. "There was a loud crack, and then my dick went soft."

Too much information, I'm thinking.

The crew at the other end of the line howled with laughter.

Eli held the phone away from his ear so I could listen.

"In that case, the doctor said you probably tore one of the main arteries in the penis. You can go to the hospital here and get medicine for the pain, but you need to fly back to the US as soon as possible. You need surgery."

As Eli finished his conversation with the captain, I looked at him and wanted to cry. I was worried he wouldn't be the same after surgery. Would he be able to get hard again? Even worse, maybe he wouldn't be able to have kids. He was only twenty-eight. This could have a huge impact on his life.

He hung up the phone, and we made plans to fly to Miami the next morning. I kept changing the ice pack during the night, praying he would be okay.

We arrived in Miami and went to the hospital, where they scheduled Eli's surgery for the following day. The doctor found a tear at the base of one of the arteries that carries blood into the penis when it's erect. When his penis hit my pelvic bone instead of entering my vagina, the impact caused it to bend. The crack we heard was the tissue tearing, and all the fluid swelling his testicles was the blood draining from his erection.

"It's called a fractured penis, and it's more common that you think," said the doctor. "You're actually the third case we've had this week. But your case is the worst."

"Really?" I said. "This happens a lot during sex?"

"Yes," said the doctor. "But the other cases this week were from other accidents. One was from a bar fight, and one got kicked by a horse."

Our case is worse than being kicked by a horse, I was thinking as the doctor left the room.

The next morning, I sat in the waiting room as Eli was prepped for surgery. I was nervous. I was fond of him – we had become good friends and lovers within a short time. I had filled out some hospital paperwork for him earlier, and it made me realize how little we really knew each other. A nurse came and got me when he was ready.

"He wants to see you before he goes into the OR."

I walked into the room as they were transferring him to a stretcher. There was an IV in his arm; he looked a little too happy, so they must have started dripping some pain meds. Eli handed me his cell and asked me to call his parents when the surgery was over. We laughed about that conversation knowing I had never met his parents. He smiled and motioned for me to lean closer to him. He gave me a kiss and took my hand. I held on until the nurses wheeled him out of the room. I followed behind him in the hallway, never losing eye contact. He had been so pale after the accident, but now the color was back in his cheeks. He looked beautiful as he disappeared into the operating room. Just before the doors shut behind him, he mouthed "I love you", and then he was gone. That was the first time he said it to me. He couldn't see that I said it too.

While I waited, a call came through on his cell. I answered, thinking it might be his parents. It was a girl's voice. My heart sank.

Hearing her voice made me remember he was not my boyfriend. We never spoke about being exclusive. It probably was just the drugs talking when he said he loved me. I'm glad he didn't hear me say it back.

"He's busy right now, but I'll give him the message," I said. I didn't reveal anything more.

"Okay, please tell him I called," she said.

Surgery went an hour longer than expected. I spent most of that hour thinking about who the girl was and felt tempted to go through the numbers and texts on his phone. Then I went back to praying he would be okay.

I was relieved to see the doctor smiling when he came out to see me. The surgery lasted five hours.

"It went better than I expected. It was a deep tear," said the doctor. "It took longer to sew him up, because the tissue is delicate, and I wanted to leave as little scar tissue as possible. I expect him to heal fully."

I thanked him.

"It's very important he doesn't have an erection for eight to ten weeks while he heals," said the doctor. "It's natural for men to have eight to fifteen erections during the day, including when they are asleep. Eli may even have more because he's young. When he gets an erection during the night, he'll wake up, because it will hurt when it puts pressure on the stitches. Just wave smelling salts under his nose, or put a bag of ice on his penis, and it will keep it down so the stitches can heal."

I hadn't thought about Eli's recovery. My kids were coming home in two days. He couldn't go back to the boat, and he wouldn't be able to work for several weeks. I called his parents. A man's voice picked up the phone right away. It was his Dad.

"Hi, it's Betsy," I said. My voice was shaking. "I'm Eli's…friend. He's out of surgery. The doctor said everything went well, and he'll be fine."

Before I could think about what I was saying and who I was saying it to, I continued.

"The doctor said he can't have an erection for eight to ten weeks."

The line was silent, and then I heard laughter.

"Did you hear that, Patty?" his dad chuckled. I realized his mom was on the line too.

"These things only happen to Eli," she said giggling.

My face was bright red with embarrassment.

"I'll have him call you when he's out of the recovery room," I said. I was desperate to get off the line so I didn't have to talk anymore.

"Ok, and we look forward to meeting you," said his dad.

"Thanks for taking care of him," said his mom.

"Ok, bye," I said.

Eli's cell rang again immediately. I recognized the number. It was the girl who had called earlier. I turned off his phone and walked down the hall towards the recovery room. I couldn't wait to see him.

As he healed, Eli and I were forced to move beyond the physical part of our relationship. We couldn't have sex, so we talked. We learned more about each other in those few weeks than we had in four months of dating. I shared my favorite movies with him. He shared his favorite music with me. We read books together.

He made me slow down. He was healing, and it started to feel like parts of me were, too.

For my birthday a few weeks after his surgery, Eli packed a picnic, and we ate in a park overlooking the bay near my house. I walked by the park every day, but had never stopped to enjoy it. I laughed when I opened my present. It was the sort of backpack you take when you go camping. I preferred nice hotels.

At the end of two months, we took a trip to Arizona and hiked a mountain together. He took me up a challenging trail I would never have hiked before I met him. When we came down from the mountain, he got hard, and instead of reaching for a bag of ice to stop the erection, he reached for me. We made love – slowly, carefully – for the first time since his surgery. His cock was as strong as ever. I was not especially spiritual, but with Eli after the accident, sex felt sacred and reverent, maybe because I didn't take it for granted anymore. He moved his cock gently in and out of me. At first it was out of concern for his healing stitches, and then the movement became like prayer, as if our energies were joined in worship. I wasn't having an orgasm, but I was feeling something, a remembering in my body and mind.

It was amazing, but still a part of me started to push him away. I wasn't used to feeling so much love. For many years I'd trained my body not to feel, and now it was unnerving and vulnerable to feel too much. The secrets from my childhood were coming back into my memory; I didn't want to acknowledge them, but it was becoming harder to ignore them.

A month later, Eli started dreaming bigger dreams again, and he told me he was going to travel with a buddy in Australia. He said he would be gone a month. Even though I didn't mean it, I told him it was okay to stay longer.

I dropped him off at the airport, and we kissed goodbye. As I drove away, I thought about dreaming bigger dreams, too, but when I got home, I put the backpack in the storage room. It would be a few more years before I was ready to use it. At the time, I didn't realize how much I was resisting letting love in because I didn't feel I deserved it.

*"I think – from my own life experience, and certainly what I've discovered in many women and men across the planet – is [that] when we're traumatized, when we're beaten, when we're raped, we leave our bodies. We disconnect from ourselves. And if it's true that one out of every three women on the planet have been raped or beaten, which is a U.N. statistic, that's a billion women."*
—Eve Ensler

For several years after Eli left, I only dated men who were unavailable. They were emotionally distant; they would fuck me and leave. One was married. Some of the men I dated tried to make love to me, but I closed my eyes and shut them out. I kept blaming the men for leaving me, but really, I wasn't showing up for myself. I also found myself wrong for thinking the childhood incidents mattered. They were a rape of my innocence, but they weren't rape. And then, one night when I was 40, it was rape.

I was at a party with friends. It was a birthday celebration, so I knew most everyone at the party. I was introduced to Christian, a friend of the birthday boy. He was an attractive lawyer visiting from LA. At first, Christian was almost shy; he had a quiet charisma, but with alcohol in him, he became more open. We talked and then separated and then talked again throughout the evening. Late in the night, he pulled me into a room, closed the door and started kissing me. Because he'd been so reserved at first, his aggression surprised me. His kiss felt forced and out-of-control. I liked the attention from him, but I immediately pulled away, trying to slow him down. I could tell he was really drunk. He pushed me down onto the bed. I kept hoping he was being playful, but his behavior was feeling threatening. It all happened very quickly. He climbed on top of me, held my arms down with his legs, unzipped his pants and forced his cock in my mouth. I could barely breathe. I couldn't move beneath him. I turned my head away and asked him to stop.

"But I like you," he said.

He kept pressing his cock towards my closed mouth, dragging it along my cheeks as I turned my head back and forth trying to avoid being penetrated. I could feel his knees digging into my upper arms.

When his cock went soft, he got off me and lay next to me, with his arm draped over me, holding me in place. We were still for a few minutes. I was relieved he'd stopped, but too afraid to move or speak. I wished someone from the party would walk in and find us so I'd have the courage to leave. Then he started kissing me again, his tongue attacking deep into my mouth. I put my hands on his shoulders, trying to press him away. He rolled on top of me and pulled up my dress.

"No," I said.

"Just enjoy it," he whispered.

I tried to wiggle out from under him. He held me down and forced his cock inside me.

"Please stop," I said.

"I know you like it," he said. "I can tell by your face."

Was that how he interpreted my tears?

I wanted to spit at him.

I wanted to scream.

Instead, I gave in and took it because I didn't want to ruin the party. It was easy to do, because I'd spent my life not speaking up and then pretending everything was okay. I couldn't feel anything, anyway. For years, not allowing myself to feel was protection. The night I was raped, I didn't feel a thing.

After that night, it seemed clear that ignoring my history of assault was creating more abusive situations in my life; it was time to pay attention to it. I wanted to stop being a victim, but I didn't know how to speak up or who to even tell the story to. I didn't know how to fix me.

My daughter was twelve at the time. I was watching her come of age as I stayed disconnected from my own essence. What kind of role model was I?

She was excited to tell me when she got her first period. We celebrated at a favorite restaurant. Looking at her over dinner, I realized I would be disappointed if she ever felt the same shame I felt about my body and parts of my life.

I wanted her to honor and adore her body. I wanted her to speak up if she ever felt unsafe. I wanted her to feel valued as a girl and then as a woman. I wanted her to love herself. And, I knew that to be an example for her, I would have to find a way to live it.

# FOUR
## FINDING MY VOICE

*"I write for those women who do not speak, for those who do not have a voice because they were so terrified, because we are taught to respect fear more than ourselves. We've been taught that silence would save us, but it won't."*
—Audre Lorde

I spent so much of my life lying about orgasm that I didn't share the news of finally feeling my orgasm with my closest friends. Where would I even start to tell the story? I had never mentioned being molested when I was younger. How much of my truth did I want to reveal?

I told a few people I was doing orgasm research, but I made a joke about it. They joked about it, too. It made me sorry I wasn't brave enough to tell the whole story. I felt like I was dishonoring my newly discovered orgasm, my vagina and my body by making the jokes.

While I was finally comfortable feeling the truth in my body, I was not comfortable speaking the truth. Maybe the young girl inside was still concerned about being judged. I spent so much of my life not speaking up, and when I did, I usually said what I thought the other person wanted to hear, not speaking my truth.

I decided to sign up for a private Extended Massive Orgasm (EMO) session with Steve Bodansky to continue my orgasm research. I had heard him speak when I took a course with Regena Thomashauer. Steve was a master of orgasms. A big paradigm shift for me about orgasm was his belief (and that of many sex teachers and orgasm experts) that all pleasurable sensations during intimacy are part of orgasm. Your orgasm can begin with the first stroke, or even before someone touches you. It can start with the kiss; just thinking about someone can throw your body into an orgasmic state. The climax, which I used to equate to orgasm, is when you actually go over the edge and get a full body release. Most of us are so focused on the outcome, the climax, that we don't enjoy and honor all the amazing sensations of our orgasm.

Steve usually does EMO sessions, which focus only on stroking the clit, with his wife Vera at their home in Northern California. This time, though, he was working with Wendy, a woman in New York City, offering private sessions in EMO.

It was a cold day in November, but as I walked to Wendy's apartment on the Upper West Side, my back and thighs were clammy with sweat. I was nervous. I had heard Steve speak, but I'd never met him or Wendy, and I was about to be in bed with them.

Wendy welcomed me into her home, and we sat with Steve for a few minutes in her living room while they briefed me on what to expect during the hour-long session. She looked familiar.

"First, you'll watch Steve do me," said Wendy in her soft voice. Her dark curls framed her porcelain skin and full lips. She was about my age. On the wall behind her was a poster of a recent award-winning film. I realized she was a filmmaker, like me, and it occurred to me that this would make a great scene in a Woody Allen film.

I nodded as if I were completely comfortable with the set-up, but I felt my vagina clamp shut. I asked about her current film project to delay going into the bedroom.

During the EMO sessions, the giver (Steve) stays fully clothed and sits in an upright position, usually on a bed. The receiver lies on the bed, undressed from the waist down. This was way beyond my comfort zone.

Steve and Wendy asked me to meet them in her bedroom when I was ready. I went into the bathroom to change into my robe. I felt like I might faint. I slowly took off my clothes, put on my robe and then looked at my face in the mirror. *Who was I? Why was I doing this?* I felt such disapproval for the woman looking back at me in the mirror.

Steve was sitting at the head of the bed, his back propped up by one of Wendy's pretty silk pillows. Wendy was lying across the bed horizontally in front of him. His right leg was draped gently over her chest. His left leg fell open on the bed. It looked like a position you might use while you do a puzzle or play a game of monopoly, but instead of a board, the focus was on Wendy's genitals. They invited me to join them on the bed. I sat at the end of the bed as far away as possible.

"Why don't you move a little closer?" Wendy suggested. I scooted forward towards the center of the bed, trying to keep my robe from falling open.

Steve's hands softly rubbed her thighs. He said it was to ground her and to connect with her energy. Wendy's robe was open at the waist, and her legs were butterflied open. Her cheeks were already flushed.

"Do you see her outer labia are already becoming engorged?" said Steve.

I turned my gaze towards her abdomen, but my eyes darted away to the window. This felt weird. *What am I doing here?* I thought. I don't want to look at another woman's vagina.

Steve put on latex gloves, which are recommended unless you are in a committed relationship with the stroker. Steve and Wendy weren't lovers. He was only using her as a demo for the EMO session.

He opened a jar of lube and took a small dollop on the tip of his right index finger. His slow movements and focus reminded me of a priest preparing the Eucharist. His left hand slid under her butt with his thumb resting at the bottom of her vulva. He spent a minute looking at her genitals.

"Beautiful," he said. "Your lips are becoming a deep red. The outer lips are swelling as more blood flows to the area. I'm going to touch you now."

Wendy nodded.

My heart was racing.

Steve placed his finger with the lube at the bottom of her vulva and took a slow upwards stroke.

Wendy sighed.

The lips on her face parted into a smile.

As he stroked her, I was surprised to feel my vagina get wet.

"Now I'm going to move the hood so you can see her clit," said Steve. "Do you see it?"

This time I didn't look away. Her clit was a soft pink and shaped like a pearl. It reminded me of mine. All my life, I heard about how hard it is for men to find the clit, but once again, I was surprised to see it really isn't hard to find if you take time to look at the anatomy.

"During EMO we focus on the upper left quadrant of the clit where there is the most sensation," Steve said as he moved his finger to just above the spot. "This is where I'm going to focus my strokes."

I nodded. My mind shifted from judgment about being in the room with a half-naked woman I didn't know to anticipation of what would happen next. I was suddenly fascinated with the female anatomy.

He began stroking her, using the lightest of strokes and motion.

"Yes," she moaned. "That's good."

Steve's eyes stayed on her genitals.

Stroke by stroke by stroke, like he was in a trance, his finger caressed only a small area of her clit.

Her vulva shimmered with a combination of the lube and her own juices, each contraction making the area more luminous. I felt a quiver in my belly, and my vagina was moist. None of it felt sexual to me, it felt sensual. I didn't feel desire to be with either of them, but I was aware of my own turn-on, something I'd suppressed in the past.

Steve quickened his strokes.

"I'm going to take her to a peak," he said. His strokes got shorter and faster. My heartbeat quickened as I watched him, but my breath stayed long and deep just like Wendy's.

Every breath pulled a shiver of excitement through my body. It was weird. I could feel her orgasm. Suddenly, being in a room exploring my sensuality with two strangers felt so much more authentic than being in bed with a lover and not speaking up about my desires.

After fifteen minutes, he ended her session by taking his hand and pressing it firmly over her pubic bone to bring her down from her orgasm.

Now it was my turn.

I was nervous again.

I wanted to leave.

I wondered why it was easier for me to cheer Wendy on in her orgasm than to take responsibility for mine.

Steve changed his gloves and put a fresh towel on the bed. He motioned for me to lie with my ass on the towel. Wendy took my place in the middle of the bed.

I lay down and kept my knees together. My breathing was shallow.

"I'm going to touch you now, okay?" Steve said.

I nodded.

"I want you to speak up and say yes or no. Let's have verbal communication, okay?"

I nodded again, then remembered.

"Yes," I said.

Steve put his hand on my left thigh.

"Can you butterfly your legs open?"

I pushed the soles of my feet together and let my thighs drop to each side.

I felt exposed. It was not just my nakedness.

Wendy and Steve placed pillows under each thigh. Their focus was already on my vagina.

I felt sick.

This was wrong.

I wanted to cry.

"I'm nervous," I said as I closed my eyes to calm myself, trying to disappear into the movie in my head.

"It's okay," said Wendy. She placed a hand on my right shoulder. He touch calmed me. It was like having a life preserver nearby in case anything went wrong.

"Try and keep your eyes open. It helps you stay connected."

"I'm going to massage your thighs to get you grounded," said Steve

I nodded.

He waited.

"Okay," I said.

Steve pressed down on my upper thighs with the heels of his hands I could feel a surge of heat with each compression.

My head was spinning with stories.

I don't know them. I'm undressed in a bed with two strangers in NYC. Maybe I don't really care to find my orgasm. Maybe life is okay the way it is. Maybe I'm crazy. Maybe sex is okay without getting off. Maybe I should give up sex. Do normal people do this?

"I'm going to look at your pussy now," said Steve.

In his book, he calls this noticing. It's observing without judgment.

"Your clit is already peeking out of the hood. You have a freckle on your inner right thigh. The outer lips are turning a deep shade of burgundy."

My heart tightened. It was the first time anyone had ever commented on my genitals. All of the air in my next breath went straight to my heart and I could feel the veins pulse and expand.

"Beautiful," said Wendy.

I felt woozy like I did when I was hiking and looked over a cliff, feeling anxious that gravity was going to pull me over. Whenever that happens, I look directly in front of me and focus only on the next step. Step by step until I'm free from danger.

Steve rested his arm on my leg as he unscrewed the top of the lube jar and dipped his right index finger into the gel.

"I'm going to hold my hand over your genitals. Tell me if you feel anything," he said.

Within seconds, I felt heat even though he wasn't touching me. *Was it coming from his hand or from my vagina?*

"Do you feel anything?"

I smiled, and then realized that wasn't enough. I spoke quietly.

"It feels warm, like I'm next to a heater. And the warmth feels like it's spreading all over this area." I waved my hand above my abdomen.

"Good. You're already tumescent. Your body is responding so well."

That made me smile.

It was exciting to hear my body was responding.

"I'm going to touch you now."

He never took his eyes off my genitals, like the conversation he was having was strictly between him and my vagina.

"Thank you," I said, hearing myself but wondering where the voice came from. I couldn't believe I was about to let a random man touch my clit with a random woman watching.

My eyes started to close, but I forced them open. I didn't know where to look, so I looked at the ceiling and then to Steve. He stayed focused on my genitals.

He stroked the inside of my legs.

He stroked the area around my vulva.

He stroked everywhere except my vagina.

I wanted to pull him on top of me and make him do more.

My body was throbbing

"I'm going to pull your outer labia apart," he said.

I said "yes" right away.

A rush of coolness came up through my throat as he delicately opened the lips. A tingle followed. It made me quiver.

"Wow. That feels so good," I said, raising my head up astonished. "I've never had that done to me before."

I dropped my head to the bed as his finger took a long stroke upward from my perineum to just before my clit. The warmth of my vagina turned the lube to liquid instantly, and it ached for more.

"I see you're already having contractions. You're very orgasmic."

His words sent a zing through my body and mind. It felt like truth realigning in my cells. For years, I turned off my brain from feeling any pleasure. I didn't feel it was safe to receive it. I didn't feel I deserved it. After so much damage, it was good to hear from an expert that I was still orgasmic without using a vibrator.

My eyes filled with water. I squeezed them shut to stop the tears. Wendy brushed my shoulder.

"Try to keep your eyes open," she said. "It helps you stay present. Let yourself feel everything."

For years, I closed my eyes to disconnect from everything around me, even when I was having sex, even from the person I was having it with.

"I'm going to stroke your clit now," said Steve.

The tip of his finger delivered short, light strokes on one spot of my clit. It was a micro-movement in an area smaller than the tip of a pencil eraser, but that tiny move flooded my body with a wave of ecstasy.

"That's so good," I sighed.

"Do you want me to stroke faster or slower?" asked Steve.

I just want you to do me, I thought. You're the expert. I've waited so long to feel this, I just want to lie back and get off.

"Both feel good," I said as I was thinking, *why do we have to talk?*

"I want you to tell me what you want for the next stroke, faster or slower?"

He was not letting me tune him out.

He was making me become the expert on my body.

He was making me ask for what I wanted.

It made me hate him for a second.

And then I checked in with my body and spoke up.

"I like it slower," I said. The response surprised me because to me sex was better when it was faster, harder. That's mostly what I knew. That's how most men fucked me.

"Like that?" he said as he made an adjustment to his stroke.

"Yes, thank you," I sighed, relieved to have listened to my body.

Instantly I was rewarded. A new feeling came with the change of stroke. It was like he was playing an instrument, and I just heard a new note.

The slower stroke made me feel even more of the orgasm.

I kept my eyes open even though they felt like they were rolling back into my head. My orgasm kept taking me to new places. More notes, more sensation… The music kept expanding.

Now, I was ready for more, I wanted to ask him to go faster.

"I'm going to take you to a peak, okay?"

It felt like he was reading my mind. He didn't wait for me to answer. His strokes got shorter and quicker. I felt a buzz.

"Yes, yes, yes," I whispered. "That feels amazing."

"Good, Betsy," I heard Wendy say.

I had forgotten she was there.

My breath shortened with the faster strokes. I clenched my hands.

"Relax into it," he said. "Push out through your pussy."

It was the opposite of my instinct, but I followed his directions. I could feel even more.

"Okay, I'm going to take you back down," said Steve.

Nooooo, I thought. I wanted to keep floating higher. The drug was too good.

I looked at Steve and kept quiet. I trusted the trip he was taking me on.

The strokes went back to being longer and slower, but I was surprised that as I came down from the peak, the sensation continued to amplify instead of disappearing. My clit felt like it had turned from a drop of rain into one of the Great Lakes. Each stroke was sending more of the elixir through me.

"That feels really good. Can you go faster, please," I said.

"You want more?" said Steve. "You ready for another peak?"

"Please."

I was already higher than ever before.

I couldn't feel his finger on me; instead, I felt a wave of energy between us.

If I wanted it, it was there.

I only needed to ask for what I wanted.

My body pulled the energy in.

"Thank you. So good. Thank you."

"Good, Betsy," Steve said. "Beautiful. You deserve this."

The tears started to flow.

Yes, I deserved this. And I was safe.

After the third time of taking my orgasm to a peak, Steve ended the session by cupping his hand over my genitals to bring me down from the sensations. I came back into my body, but still felt a buzzing everywhere. I could have gone on forever. My clit was throbbing with desire.

After he lifted his hand, he looped his arm through mine to help me to a sitting position. We talked about the peaks of my orgasm and how to communicate with a partner during sex.

"When you self-pleasure, keep researching what your body likes, so you can let your partner know," he said. "And then ask for what you want."

I was dating a man, Wes, but we hadn't slept together. I was feeling more confident in my orgasm, and the EMO experience made me want to explore more with a lover.

Wes was an entertainment agent. He was ten years younger than I, looked like Harry Connick Jr. and was very charming. I had no problem getting turned on around him. We both travelled a lot, so most of our intimate conversations were when we lay in our beds in different cities as we spoke on the phone. One weekend, soon after my EMO session, we both ended up in LA. I decided I wanted to have sex.

Before I met him for dinner, I took a hot bath and filled the tub with bubbles, scented oils and desires. I carefully put on lotion, noticing each area I caressed. I still avoided looking in a full length mirror. I could appreciate my body piece by piece, but my image of how I looked and how I was supposed to look in order for a man to like me echoed in my head. It was something my oldest sister Susan had taught me when I was a teenager.

I was a swimmer from the age of eight to eighteen. As my body was coming of age, my swim coach had us copy the training of the East German swimmers who were winning the Olympic medals. They were doing heavy weights on slow repetition, so we did, too. My thin legs and shoulders became strong with muscle. I was fourteen. By the time I quit swimming, my body was bulkier than most girls my age, but I loved the way it felt in the water. I felt powerful.

Both of my sisters were cheerleaders and county fair queens. My oldest sister, Susan, was seven years older than I. Sharon was four years older. I was ten when Susan was crowned the fair queen. I would sneak into her room and try on her crown, imagining what it would feel like to be the queen, to be her. A few years later, Susan was home for the summer, and I was telling her about a new guy I'd met who showed interest at first and then stopped calling. I was sixteen.

"Guys don't like bodies like yours," she said.

"What do you mean?" I said.

"You're too big. You're too strong, too much muscle."

I hunched my shoulders over, trying to get smaller. It was the first time I remember being ashamed of how I looked, and it came from someone I'd always wanted to be like – my older sister, my model.


When I was seeing Wes, it was thirty years later, and I had given birth to five children. My body no longer resembled an East German swimmer, but the imprint of Susan's comment had stuck with me for years. I wondered why some words stick, and some words are easy to release.

After dinner, Wes and I held hands as we got into a cab and went back to my hotel room. He started kissing me as soon as we were in the room.

His full lips were warm pressed against my mouth.

He held my face as his tongue traced my lips.

His hard cock pulsed against my thigh through his pants.

I could feel the wetness of my vagina underneath my black dress.

He gently laid me on the bed.

I pulled him to me to continue kissing, but instead he went straight to his belt and then his zipper.

I could feel contractions in my vagina. This is nice, I'm thinking. I'm already orgasmic, and it didn't take loads of foreplay.

He pulled off his pants, lowered himself over me and guided his cock to my mouth.

This is going too quickly, I thought.

I wasn't ready to put him in my mouth; I wanted to keep kissing him.

I opened my mouth and took him in.

"That's good, baby," he said as he pushed himself in and out of my mouth.

My vagina was aching for attention.

I glided my fingers across his balls, stroking the area between his ass and testicles.

"You are so good," he moaned. He put his hand on my head. It felt like he was holding me down.

I pulled my mouth off his cock just before he rolled over and came. I watched his sperm stream over his abs. I didn't feel a thing in my genitals.

"Thank you baby," he said. "You're amazing."

I smiled like everything was okay.

He pulled me into him and closed his eyes. I wanted to ask him to stroke my clit, to kiss, to enjoy my body. Instead, I kept my mouth shut.

My throat tightened when I heard him snoring. I moved my body away from him until we weren't touching. The next morning, I got up early and told him I had a meeting. He dressed and asked when we could see each other again. I smiled and kissed him. I pretended everything was fine. I think he thought it was.

After he left, I shut the door and fell into bed. I thought about Lea's letter mentioning my lack of zeal in bed. I thought about how quickly my vagina shut down when Wes guided me to give him a blow job. I loved giving head, but I felt too rushed with Wes. I suddenly realized the problem wasn't my lack of zeal, the problem was me not speaking up. It was me, not staying connected to what my desires were, not listening to my body. I had finally opened my body to feeling again, but I still wasn't asking for what I wanted. How was Wes supposed to know what I wanted, if I didn't ask?

# FIVE
# FALLING IN LOVE

*"We are the ones we've been waiting for."*
—Hopi Elders

I thought that feeling my orgasm would be the hard part for me, but clearly asking for what I wanted was the bigger issue that was keeping me from enjoying sex with a partner. I felt sure the voice of the little girl who didn't speak up when she was abused lay buried inside of me.

I signed up for a series of Pleasure Intensives (PI) with Regena Thomashauer and her PI partner, John. They were going to coach me in intimacy and sensuality during orgasm. There would be three of us sharing the bed.

My intention for the sessions was to continue expanding my ability to feel my orgasm while being comfortable speaking up and letting a partner know what felt good for my body.

"How's your pussy today?" Regena yelled gleefully when I walked through the door of her home office on the lower east side in NYC. I laughed at her exuberance. I felt like Dorothy in the Wizard of Oz. I was not in Indiana anymore.

I had come a long way with my orgasm since first taking her course through the School of Womanly Arts. I had been conditioned to ignore and be ashamed of my own essence. I was finally appreciating being a woman.

I never used the word pussy until I met Regena. To me, pussy was as offensive as saying cunt. Those two words simply weren't in my vocabulary, and if I heard them, I felt they were degrading to women. When I did speak of my genitals, I only referred to my vagina, which was the internal canal; vulva would probably have been more accurate. But mostly, I didn't have a name for my genitals at all. They were nameless.

I changed into a robe and joined Regena and John on Regena's bed. John was fully clothed, sitting in the same vertical position Steve Bodansky had used in our session. Regena lay next to him with her legs open. They were going to demo an extended massive orgasm (EMO) for me.

It was my second time to see another woman's vulva up close.

The first time was when I had seen Wendy's during the session with Steve. At that time, I didn't fully appreciate the beauty of a woman's genitals. By the time I worked with Regena, I looked at her vulva with fascination and gratitude for the gift of being born a woman.

John pulled back her hood to show her pink clit; it was the color of a seashell.

*Beautiful*, I thought.

John pointed with his finger.

"Touch the upper left area," he said.

I moved my hand to just above her pussy.

I could feel heat from both of us.

Regena sighed.

I placed my finger on her clit.

"Mmmm," she moaned.

The touch made me realize how far I'd come from my feelings of shame and judgment.

I held my finger there without moving.

The room was quickly filling with a thick electric energy. It reminded me of the stillness of the air in Indiana just before a lightning storm.

"Our clit holds 8,000 nerve endings," Regena reminded me. "We are wired for pleasure."

I smiled and slowly pulled my finger away, still feeling the connection shooting up into my hand and arm.

I sat on the bed like a yogi as I watched John begin stroking Regena. It was like watching a guitar virtuoso playing his favorite instrument. Because they were also occasional lovers, John knew Regena's body well. He seduced her orgasm out of her by playing a symphony of notes on her clit, each delivered at just the right spot with just the right intensity.

I could feel Regena's energy expand beyond her body. It was as if the orgasm was taking control of the space around her. During the session with Steve and Wendy, I was nervous about being stroked. With Regena and John, I couldn't wait for her demo to be over so I could lie down and receive.

I loved that my orgasm was getting greedy.

It made me think about what I wanted from a man, beyond sharing an orgasm. I wanted deep connection. I wanted him to think with his heart. I wanted him to appreciate nature. I wanted him to appreciate me.

"Betsy, you ready?"

"Betsy?"

John's face was turned away from me.

I have trouble hearing. It's another secret I don't tell about myself. I'm slowly going deaf.

"What?" I said. "Sorry, it's hard for me to hear unless I'm looking right at you."

"Do you tell the men you're dating about your hearing?" asked Regena.

"No. And it was actually when I was in bed with a man that I realized I might have a problem," I said, and I continued the story.

A few years ago, I was giving a blow job to Paul, a man I had been dating for several months. When we were intimate, it was usually in well-lit places. In my bed with the afternoon sun streaming through the windows. On a daybed next to a fire pit in a lush Miami garden. On the beach in the Bahamas under the moonlight.

Two months into seeing him, we were in a hotel room in Los Angeles. It was late at night, and the shades were pulled. My mouth was around his cock, energetically sucking. I could hear Paul saying something. I murmured as if I understood, but I didn't. I focused on rapidly bringing him in and out of my mouth, almost as if I were trying to keep the lead in a race. He kept speaking, his words a mumble to me. Finally, he gently tugged at my arm and pulled me to him. I could barely see his lips moving in the dark.

"Can you go slower?" he said.

Flustered, I made my way back down to his cock and finished. Slowly.

The next time we made love, I made sure the lights were on.

As our relationship was ending, I finally told him I was having trouble hearing.

He began speaking louder and slower to me, like I was a child or someone who had trouble following directions.

After Paul, I dated a man named Alex. When we had sex, I made sure there was always enough light so I could understand what he was saying. I don't know why I was afraid to tell him I couldn't hear well. Perhaps I didn't want him to yell at me like Paul did after he found out. Instead, I frequently said "what?" so I had another chance to decipher what he was saying.

One night at dinner, I was having trouble hearing Alex. We were sitting across from each other at an extra-long table for two beneath a speaker playing music. Between swigs of red wine, Alex talked about his divorce and how hard it was to open himself up to love again. He reached across the table and took one of my hands. I strained to read his wine-stained lips. Alex spoke about what he wanted in a relationship and how much he enjoyed our time together. I moved the candle closer to Alex just as the restaurant lowered the lighting for the evening diners. My eyes focused on Alex's mouth. He said something and then stopped talking.

I wasn't sure, but I thought he said "I love you".

I wasn't ready to hear these words from him yet. I didn't say "what?" this time. Instead, just as I did with Paul, I murmured. It wasn't a yes or a no, just a sound of acknowledgment.

He stared at me waiting for more. I stared back. He was quiet the rest of the meal. I didn't mind the silence. It was easier than talking about my real feelings.

I finally booked an appointment to see a hearing specialist. The doctor ran a series of tests and reviewed my family history. My grandfather lost most of his hearing in his 90s. I was forty-four.

"You have congenital hearing loss in both your ears," the doctor said.

"So I'm going deaf? And in both ears?"

"Maybe not completely, but you'll continue to lose your hearing. The good news is hearing aids will improve what you can hear."

The doctor asked me to choose a color for the portion of the hearing aid that would be visible around my ear. I chose the shade closest to my skin tone, rather than bright pink or a purple leopard print, which were both options. Like so many of the things in life I didn't want to acknowledge, I wanted my hearing aids to be invisible.

Three weeks later, I picked up my hearing aids. Even though they were tiny and lightweight, they felt huge, foreign and uncomfortable in my ears, like having a piece of sand in my eye. The assistant showed me how to change the volume and the batteries. I left the office wearing my new 'ears', but within in an hour, I turned the volume down. I was hearing too much.

I wore my hearing aids for four months, but every day I wore them less and less. First, I tried turning the volume way down. Then I tried wearing only one. When I kissed the man I was dating, I took them out because I wanted to feel his hands holding my face without being concerned he would rub against them. Mostly, I found that I preferred not hearing well to hearing everything.

Regena was lying in John's arms, staring at me as I finished the story. "Ok, so you have to practice on me."

"Practice what?" I said, surprised, thinking she wanted me to stroke her clit. This was not what I paid for!

"Pretend I'm the man you're dating, and tell him you're losing your hearing."

I cringed.

"How?"

"Lean into him and tell him how to speak to you, so you can hear every word he says."

Regena moved in close to my ear and whispered the last part: "Seduce him with the information."

The words dripped off her tongue like a candle melting. What a tease.

"Ok, I got it." I laughed.

"Then give it to me," she said.

She sat up, waiting.

She was completely naked.

John was sitting up next to her.

"Now?" I said.

"Yes, now. We aren't going to start your session until you pretend I'm a man you want to fuck, and you tell me you're going deaf."

I got up from the bed and stood in front of her in my robe.

"I have something to tell you," I said quietly.

"What's that?" said Regena, changing her tone like she had balls.

"I'm losing my hearing, so when you talk to me, I need to see your lips."

Regena smiled.

"Good," she said. "Now this time, I want you to send energy to your pussy first, and then tease me with your words. Make hearing loss the sexiest thing ever!"

Fuck, I thought. Okay, I'll try again, even though this seems so crazy to be seducing a naked woman pretending to be a man with my story of losing my hearing. I just wanted to feel my orgasm. What does this have to do with getting off?

I moved closer to the edge of the bed and got down on my knees in front of her and put my hands on her bare thighs.

I looked her in the eyes and spoke slightly above a whisper. John disappeared into the background. I smiled as I thought about how much my vulva looked like a beautiful flower, and then I started speaking.

"I'm losing my hearing," I said. "It's something I was born with."

I took a breath to stay connected to myself and to her.

"Instead of wearing hearing aids, I prefer to read lips. So when I'm with you, please make sure I can see your mouth."

I moved in closer.

"You don't have to talk louder," I whispered as I stared into her eyes.

"You. Just. Need. To. Look. At. Me."

Regena's mouth broke into a huge smile.

"Excellent, Bets," she said. "That's it. Just enjoy yourself while you're telling him. It doesn't matter what you are saying as long as you are saying it from your turn-on."

"Thank you," I said. It felt good to speak up.

"Now, let's practice speaking up about what your pussy wants."


*"Freedom is from within."*
—Frank Lloyd Wright


Once I discovered my orgasm, I didn't want to pretend anymore. I wanted to feel the truth in my body, which meant I needed to speak that truth as well.

I did three sessions with Regena and John.

It was surprising how much healing happened just by allowing myself to feel my orgasm. It wasn't just healing my vagina, it was also healing my voice.

I'd had a history of extreme sore throats for years, and they suddenly disappeared when I started connecting to my orgasm and speaking up about what truth felt like in my body.

"Tell me how you want to be stroked," John asked. "Be specific."

I was lying next to him with my legs butterflied open.

Regena was sitting on the bed next to me.

"I would like long, slow strokes," I said.

He started caressing as soon as I spoke. His finger just grazed the delicate skin on the tip of my clit. I was still getting used to how much more I felt when the touch was lighter.

"That's good. Thank you. That feels really good. Now can you make small circles around my clit?"

John changed his stroke and I was instantly rewarded with a new sensation.

"Amazing. So good. Thank you."

I didn't have to think about what I wanted. My body was feeding me the answers. For the first time, I was in control of my orgasm. I was listening to my body, and my body was taking me to new places because I was asking for it.

"Can you go a little faster now?" I said. "And change between circles and short strokes."

John changed his movement before I finished speaking. It's like he knew where I was going before I asked.

"Wow. Thank you," I said in wonder of the new sensations my body was experiencing.

Just when I thought I'd felt the greatest expression of my orgasm, I would breath in and feel even more, the expansion taking me further into ecstasy and beyond my previous experiences of orgasm. I thought less about trying to climax during orgasm and more about surrendering to feeling everything. The tickle in my clit, the flutter of contractions in my vagina, the flush of warmth in my belly, the tingling in my toes and the surge of endorphins stimulating my mind took me naturally into a higher state of receiving. At times, I felt like I was floating outside my body. It reminded me of the weightlessness and serenity I'd felt during my near death experience several years earlier. My mind, body and spirit were fully open to feeling everything.

Suddenly, I had trouble breathing. John's strokes slowed down. It was becoming harder to draw a full breath into my lungs.

"Pull your breath all the way through, Betsy," Regena whispered. "Inhale from your pelvis all the way up to the top of your head and then exhale all the way down."

I turned to look at her, trying to trust what she was telling me – I felt like I was suffocating.

She put one of her hands just above my pubic bone and one hand on my head as guides for my breath. I inhaled deeper as tears poured from my eyes, streaking down my cheeks.

Regena moved her bottom hand to my heart, so now one of her hands was on my head, and one was on my heart.

I wasn't sure what was happening.

"That's good, Bets," said Regena. "Keep breathing, stay connected. You're doing great."

I was humming with orgasm as the image of my childhood bedroom came into my mind. I wanted to slam my legs shut.

"You're okay," Regena whispered. "Stay with your breath."

My throat felt like I was being choked.

"Stay connected to your pussy," she said. "Feel everything."

John kept stroking.

My head was exploding with images and feelings of pain and pleasure, judgment and shame, hatred and sadness.

"How are you doing, Bets?" Regena said.

"It feels like too much," I heard myself saying.

"Give your body permission to feel again. Go beyond the darkness. Feel it and go beyond," Regena said.

My head was woozy with pressure, like I was going to pass out.

Take off your shorts, I remembered. Open your legs. Say nothing.

I tried to focus on the warmth coming from Regena's hands. They became my life force. I placed my hands on my stomach over my womb.

My breaths became longer and slower.

As the image of my six-year-old bedroom slipped away, so did the pain, and I inhaled a wave of pure bliss. I looked at Regena and wondered what was taking over my body.

"You are feeling the eight thousand nerve endings in your clit," she said. "It's your birthright as a woman to feel pleasure."

After the session ended, I finally found a name to honor my genitals, my *L'Origin du Monde*.

I finally fell in love with my pussy.

# SIX
# BEYOND ORGASM

*"When you see your body as holy and sacred, your entire life changes."*
—Dr. Christiane Northrup

As I researched orgasm, I started to look for ways to honor my body as sacred. It was not something that came naturally to me, because I spent most of my life not appreciating my body. When I looked in the mirror, I didn't see myself, I saw my flaws. I never approved of myself until I realized that if I didn't treat my body with love and appreciation, no one else would. It was a lesson I received over and over again, and finally I decided to pay attention and make a change.

It was a dead orchid that made me think about the consequences of not loving myself.

I had one orchid at my home in Miami. It stayed on the kitchen table until I cleaned the table, and then I'd move it to the counter. It sat on the counter until I needed the space and moved it to the window. Every so often when I watered it, some of the petals fell off into the sink. Mostly, I ignored the plant.

One day I returned from a trip and noticed all the leaves on the orchid were brown and wilted. The delicate pearl-colored petals were long gone. Even the stem was drooping and dry; the plant had lost its juiciness, its joy to live.

I took it into the kitchen to throw it away along with the junk mail that arrived during my absence. When I lifted the base of the plant out of the clay pot, I was surprised to see a web of roots, still green and plump.

It would have been easier to throw the orchid away, but instead I took time to remove the dead leaves and stem. I gently watered all the roots, paying attention to the flow of water. Not too much – I didn't want to cause more damage. I put the hydrated plant back into the pot. There was no sign of green. It seemed hopeless, but I knew there was life beneath the dirt.

It was almost bedtime, so I carried the pot to my bedside table. I got ready for bed, and for some reason as I turned off the light on my bedside table, I looked at the pot filled with dirt and said, "I love you." I fell asleep thinking I might be going a little nuts talking to a pot full of dirt and hoping my words might have some impact on its future. Maybe I should have just thrown it away.

The next morning as I woke up, I saw the pot a few feet from my head. I said "Good morning" and then "I love you" as I moved the pot to the window and opened the shades to let in the sunrise. When I wrote during the day, I moved the pot to my writing table. At night, I put it back on my bedside table. I don't know why, but I continued this pattern daily, making sure to say "I love you" to the orchid every day. Surely, I thought, I must be crazy.

After a month, a pale green stem pushed through the dirt. It continued to grow, as if remembering who it was before it nearly died. Three months later, some buds appeared on the stem. Over the next few weeks, the buds grew bigger and more numerous. The plant had come back to life.

Dr. Masaru Emoto, a Japanese writer, explored how human consciousness affects the molecular structure of water. When he placed positive words of love, appreciation and gratitude on containers of water, he noticed that the water formed beautiful microscopic crystals. When he taped negative words to the containers, the water showed up dark and muddy.

I knew my body was about 70% water. My experience with the orchid and Dr. Emoto's research made me pay closer to attention to the impact my thoughts might have on my body. For years, I'd been sending a negative loop to my cells – based on a mixture of mean comments from others and my own insecurities – and it left a thick layer of heaviness around my body. Some of it was flesh, but most of it was negative energy.

When I discovered Qoya classes, it was the first positive connection I'd felt to my body in a long time. Qoya, created by Rochelle Schieck, was a new type of movement class with ancient roots. Rochelle grew up as a dancer, later becoming a yoga teacher and then a shaman. During a trip to the jungle in Peru, Rochelle absorbed the information that became the seeds of Qoya.

In my first Qoya class, I was asked to honor my body as a temple, as holy and sacred. This was as uncomfortable for as me being asked to butterfly my legs open when I first started my orgasm research. How does someone move when she feels holy? How do I access holiness when I don't like the way my thighs look? My attitude about my body was wired for disapproval, and even as I was becoming the champion of my orgasm, I was not in love with my body.

Rochelle opened the class by inviting us to set an intention for our dance during the next two hours. My first instinct was to offer my intention to heal my family. It had been twelve years since my divorce, and my family was fractured, split between the world of my ex-husband – who'd had two more children with two different women – and myself. We didn't feel like a family anymore. We had always spent holidays together post-divorce, but this year my ex-husband asked me not to make the annual Christmas trip to Colorado, because his new girlfriend, our former nanny, was uncomfortable with me there.

"It's even better if you make the intention about yourself instead of others," Rochelle suggested, as though she had read my mind.

I switched my intention to loving my body for the next two hours, even though I believed healing for my family was more important.

We started the class by lying on our backs, and as India.Arie sang on the soundtrack in the background, Rochelle guided us through giving ourselves a massage. She encouraged us to touch ourselves like we were touching a beloved. My right hand began rubbing my left hand and wrist. I moved quickly to my arm and up towards my shoulders, already thinking of how much time I needed to get through every body part before the song ended.

"Slow down and give attention and gratitude to each area," said Rochelle. "Don't just go through the motions. Experiment with what feels good, and then see if you can find a way to make it feel even better."

Her words made me backtrack down my arm to give more attention to my forearm, which I had passed over in my rush to move ahead. Rather than rubbing, I took the tip of my fingers and traced a path from my wrist to my inner elbow. I felt butterflies in my stomach. It felt so good that I tried it again, not worried about Rochelle's invitation to move on to our shoulder and necks. I admired the freckles on my arm as my fingers glided across my skin. I outlined the tattoo on my wrist, the Hindu symbol for breath. I had gotten the tattoo a few years earlier, in memory of the time I spent holding my friend Sheri's hand as she was dying of ovarian cancer.

My fingers travelled up to explore the tightness in my shoulders. I crossed my arms so each hand could rest on the opposite shoulder. Just like Dr. Emoto placing messages on the bottles of water, I imagined sending love into the tightness. I imagined the cells being flooded with gratitude.

I moved my hands to the top of my head and enjoyed feeling the tug on my hair. And then, like wax dripping down a candle, I dragged the tips of all ten fingers down my face, stopping to explore the sensations around my eyes and cheekbones. I stroked the bumpy ridge on my nose, the result of stepping into the path of my son's swing twelve years before. I brought my hands to my throat and made light circles. I was surprised to feel my pussy pulse as I caressed my throat. They had both been closed for years.

My right hand played along my collar bone as my left hand continued towards my right breast. I admired the fleshiness of one breast and then the other. I never wore a bra growing up, I was probably an A cup so

I never needed to hold anything in. In fourth grade one of our spelling words was 'concave' and our homework assignment was to write a definition for each word. After class, one of the boys pointed to me on the playground and announced, "Betsy's chest is concave." Everyone around us laughed.

When I gave birth, I loved the new fullness as my breasts filled with milk. Each baby preferred to nurse on my left side, so by the time I finished eight years of nursing children, one breast was smaller than the other. When I was thirty-six, I made the decision to have small implants put in make my breasts more even in size. I still held judgment and shame even around that decision, so as I massaged myself in the Qoya class, I held both breasts and sent them love.

My hands danced across my stomach. I pressed my palm into my belly button, a sensitive spot where I didn't usually like to be touched. I remembered this was the original connection to my mother. We had at one time been joined together. I had still not told her the secrets from my childhood. My heart ached as I held still, and then, when I felt an openness in the ache, I moved my hand in circles around my navel, like a labyrinth going from the inside out, until I was covering my entire stomach and abdomen with a swirl of love.

"Use the rest of the song to finish your massage, exploring any areas that need extra attention," said Rochelle. "Let your body guide you."

My hands inched down to my left hip. I embraced my left thigh with both hands and sent love to it as I rubbed slowly up and down my leg. I felt the strong quad muscles that had allowed me to enjoy hikes all over the world. I remembered my dad calling me "thunder thighs" and laughing when I was a teenager, my legs growing stronger from doing weights during swim team training. I'd worn long pants as much as possible ever since. It had been thirty years. I moved to my right thigh, and as I sent love to it, I also decided to fondle it, to touch it the way I would like a lover to touch me. I skated my fingers over my flesh and felt warmth in my abdomen as I teased myself. It all felt really good. Why had I never done this before? Why did I start ignoring parts of my body when I felt damaged, shamed or judged? Why did I let other people's beliefs determine mine?

"When we come back into the wisdom of our bodies, the physical sensation of truth, our intuition, our deep inner knowing is always inside of us, not outside of us. *Inside* of us," said Rochelle. "Through Qoya we reconnect to the source of power. Through movement, we remember."

Rochelle moved the class through heart-opening and then into hip-opening exercises. Unlike most workout class rooms, in Qoya there are no mirrors. I tried to keep my eyes closed to eliminate distractions, but while we were doing the hip circles, I opened them and peeked to see if I was doing it right.

"There are no levels in Qoya." said Rochelle. "Remember, there is no way you can do it wrong, and the way you know you're doing it right is that it feels good."

I widened my stance and thrust my hips into bigger, more playful circles. *That felt better*, I thought. I opened my eyes and was surprised to see every woman in the room moving her hips in different ways. It was a liberating change from the years of workout and yoga classes, where everyone was trying to move in the same way.

"Qoya is based on the idea that you know," Rochelle said. "It's an invitation to focus less on how it looks and more on how it feels, not only as you are moving around in class, but as a metaphor for how you live. It's a reminder that all answers are within. It's the idea that you learn how to trust the physical sensation of truth in your body and follow it, like north on your compass."

We danced during the yoga flow segment. I loved the liberty of not having to follow the instructor but instead listening to where my body wanted to go. It reminded me of my orgasm research. It reminded me of the freedom and joy I'd felt dancing in the living room of my childhood home.

For the next song, Rochelle taught us a box step. For the first time in the class, she asked us to follow her lead. I noticed that I was having fun with the movement, but not enjoying it as much as when I let my body choose my next step. Just as I was getting the hang of the box step, she suddenly announced, "Now, dance outside the box! Let your body be free."

I laughed at the suggestion and danced my way outside my box. I wondered how life would have been different if I had welcomed that invitation earlier.

"Qoya is for the moments when we choose love over fear, commitment over our giving up for convenience. It's to awaken and support the parts of ourselves that can relax and trust that there is no need to worry, because everything is working out in its divine timing, and we can enjoy the journey by dancing with it," said Rochelle.

There were chills up and down my body.

*"If anything is sacred, the human body is sacred."*
—Walt Whitman

My orgasm research connected me to feeling and speaking the truth of my orgasm. If I wanted to feel my orgasm, I had to listen to my body and ask for what I wanted. Qoya connected me to the feeling of truth in my body. If I wanted to feel good, I had to listen to my body. With every class, I fell back in love with my legs and shoulders and calves and belly. I fell back in love with myself because that, finally, was my truth. It didn't feel authentic to disapprove of myself anymore, no matter what anyone else was saying to me.

Qoya showed me how to honor my body, and in the process it liberated my spirit. This new awareness allowed me to know when a decision was right, because I could feel the answer in my body. Both Qoya and my orgasm research had fine-tuned my intuition because I was focusing on listening to the wisdom within. One thing I was noticing during sex was feeling pleasure in my clit but not feeling much when a man was inside me. I was still enjoying intimacy, but I wondered if it were possible to feel the same pleasurable sensations inside my pussy.

I experimented with a Secret Ceres jamu stick, a healing product from Indonesia in the shape of a dildo that is said to stimulate and balance the hormones in the vagina.

I spread the directions on the bathroom counter as I looked at the stick. It was a white chalky wand about six inches long and as thick as a small hotdog. I ran the stick under the faucet to activate the herbs before i eased it inside me. After about a minute, I pulled it out. Using the stick was not a turn-on, but I could feel my pussy tighten from the herbs. After working with the stick for a week, I wasn't sure about the hormones being balanced, but my pussy started to feel too tight and too dry. Even though the stick was good for 300 uses, I decided put it away after one last time. As I rinsed it, some of the clay melted onto my hands. I felt the skin tightening, so I let the clay sit for a few minutes before I washed it off. I was amazed how smooth my skin looked. Without thinking about it having just been in my vagina, I began rubbing the damp stick on my face. I left the mask on for ten minutes and was thrilled when I looked in the mirror after rinsing the herbs off. My skin looked fresh and polished. After that, my herbal stick for healing my vagina also became my new favorite face mask.

The next class I took was with Saida Desilets, a holistic healer working with jade eggs, an ancient Chinese practice to heal and honor the health of a woman's genitals. The Chinese royalty used jade stones to tone and tighten the vaginal walls. They believed the practice allowed them to give and receive greater pleasure. I thought maybe it would help to heal the inside of my pussy.

The jade eggs come in various sizes. It's recommended that you start with the smallest, a bit bigger than a robin's egg, and work your way up. For the class, I decided to buy an egg that was the middle size, slightly smaller than an egg I'd cook for breakfast.

There were about thirty women in the class. Everyone undressed from the waist down and found a comfortable spot on the floor. I went to the corner and faced away from the others.

Saida dimmed the lights and guided us through a meditation to relax us. I kept the egg on my belly as she spoke. It rolled a little with each breath. The mediation was very relaxing and made me forget I was in a room full of half-naked women.

"Now put the egg at the entrance of your yoni," she purred. "Don't push. Allow your yoni to pull the egg in."

Just as I was thinking she was wacky to suggest my pussy could draw the egg inside me, I felt a tug, and it disappeared from my hand.

I smiled, thinking what a great magic trick this would make.

We practiced squeezing and releasing several muscles in the vaginal wall before she led us through another meditation. I couldn't feel the egg, but I liked the idea of it being inside me, connecting me to an ancient healing practice. When the meditation was done, Saida instructed us to bear down and push the eggs out. If that didn't work, we could reach in and remove them with our fingers. I pushed down, and my egg popped into my hand. *Ta da*!

Saida suggested we use the jade eggs daily with her guided meditations. She said as our yonis got stronger, we could wear the jade eggs throughout the day.

For the next few weeks, I enjoyed using my jade egg daily. It felt both healing and playful for my pussy. I loved the practice of pulling the egg inside me and pushing it out again.

Sometimes after doing the mediations, I would leave the egg in and go about my work before removing it several hours later. It was easy to forget it was there.

One day before leaving my hotel to meet a friend for lunch, I decided to leave the jade egg inside me for the entire day. I got dressed, inserted the egg, and then finished putting on my make-up.

It was the kind of beautiful day where all the women on the streets of New York City were wearing their summer dresses, and all the men were looking at them appreciatively. It was so nice out I decided to walk to lunch. I was wearing a long, gauzy white maxi dress. The sheer cloth encircled my legs with every step. Several men smiled as I walked by. I smiled back. After spending so much of my life wanting to be invisible, I was finally feeling safe and good when I was seen. About twenty minutes

65

into my walk down Fifth Avenue, I felt something dropping in my pussy. It was the egg. I stopped and used my vaginal muscles to pull the egg farther inside me. I started walking again, taking smaller steps and then tiny steps, but the egg came all the way out, dropping into my panties. It was hard to walk. I slowly made my way into the closest store and asked to use the bathroom. The sales person could tell it was an emergency by the way I was walking, crossing leg over leg, though she couldn't know that I was worried the egg would drop from between my legs onto the marble floor and shatter. She escorted me through the store to the nearest toilets. She must have thought I really needed to pee.

"Come back and find me in perfumes when you're done," she said. "We have some new summer fragrances."

I thanked her and locked myself in the bathroom. I removed the egg, rinsed it in the sink and tucked it into my purse. As I walked the rest of the way to lunch, I smiled, realizing I had just laid an egg on Fifth Avenue.

Along with pole dancing and burlesque classes, several friends recommended a massage therapist who focused on internal work called a sacred yoni massage. I was hesitant to book with the therapist, whom I didn't know. All the classes I'd taken focused only on touching the clit, nothing inside the vagina, but after hearing about the breakthroughs of friends who'd had the yoni massages, I decided to book a session with Curtis. He said the massage would likely last at least four hours.

When I arrived for the session, Curtis was dressed in all white. His voice was quiet. His energy was quiet. He reminded me of the Buddhist monks I met in a monastery near the India-Tibet border. They were quiet, too. Before I undressed, he told me what to expect from the massage.

"I'll start with a full body massage to relax you, then I'll move to working outside the yoni, and as your body opens, I'll begin to do internal work. We hold a lot of emotions in the tissues and muscles of our genitals. I'll be working with your body to release stuck areas."

I nodded as if I understood. My mind was blank. I couldn't even think of a good question to ask. I think that going into the session I was hoping for a quick release and four hours of mostly pleasure. *Fun research*, I thought. Now, the reality of giving a man I'd never met permission to have his fingers inside my pussy felt strange, but I noticed the thoughts were coming from my head. My body was ready.

"Sometimes women orgasm during the massage. Some women cry. Sometimes they fall asleep. Just let your body lead you," he said. "Sometimes it can be uncomfortable if I'm working in an area that is holding on to trauma. Speak up whenever you want to take a break."

I smiled, too anxious to get a word out.

"I usually use coconut oil, is that okay?" he added.

I shook my head again.

"Okay, I'll warm up the oil while you get undressed."

I pulled off and folded my clothes, laying them on a scarlet velvet chair. The room was filled with books and art. It reminded me of a 1920s Paris salon, but this was New York City in 2009, and I was looking for ways to heal my pussy and to feel more. The concern that I was about to do something wrong still intruded on my thoughts. I reminded myself to keep checking in with my body for approval rather than my mind.

I closed my eyes when Curtis walked into the room carrying a bowl of the warm oil. He started his work with a prayer or chant – I couldn't tell the difference, but I appreciated the gesture. It made me feel a little less creeped out about having his fingers inside my pussy for the next four hours.

He started with compressions on my thighs and legs, then moved up to my hips and abdomen. His energy was calm and sure. I focused on where his hands were going next.

"I'm going to start massaging outside your yoni, and then when I feel you are ready, I will begin the inner work."

I kept my eyes closed and gave him a thumbs-up.

His first touches around my vulva gave me delicious sensations. I felt warmth flood into my genitals and thighs. *I can handle four hours of feeling this*, I thought.

He continued the massage, going deeper into some of the tissues around my pussy, pressing firmly, holding and then releasing. I spread my legs wider so he could work where my upper thighs met my genitals. He varied his pressure, and I realized this was not going to be a strictly feel-good massage. Curtis was focusing on breaking up stuck areas in my body. It was like working through the hard shells of an artichoke to get to the soft heart at the center.

And then he moved his fingers inside me. My first instinct was to shut my legs and push him out. I took a breath in and tried to relax and receive the gentle touch. I remembered I was safe and could ask him to stop at any time. I was surprised how little I felt with his fingers inside me. My clit and vulva were tingling with sensation, but once he moved his work to my vagina, I didn't feel as much.

"Is it normal not to feel anything?" I blurted out, suddenly wanting the answer.

He spoke quietly, choosing his words. "It's different for everyone," he said. "Sometimes if there has been trauma, a woman will need to release the damage from the yoni."

I had not told him about my early abuse, but I had a feeling he could feel the truth in my body.

"It really helps if you focus on your breath, bringing it anywhere I am touching," he said. "The breath helps renew the tissues and brings energy to the area. The energy from your head to your heart to your yoni needs to be open to fully feel your orgasm."

He kept rubbing, working different areas inside me. I felt nothing, but I kept sending my breath into my pelvis, hoping the next breath would bring a spark of life back to my vagina. My pussy had been a path for death, for pain and violation, for betrayals, lies and disappointments. My pussy and my lack of sensuality had even been a secret joke between my best friend and my ex-husband. I thought about ending the massage early, because it didn't seem to be doing anything. I tried hard to focus on letting go of every time I had let my body be mistreated. Finally, my mind was so exhausted that I dozed off. I woke up as he was finishing. Four and a half hours had passed.

"You had lots of stuck tissues," he said. "Layers of protection. You should begin to feel more of your yoni the next time you have sex."

He bowed before he walked out of the room.

I got dressed and left, unsure what to do next. Deep inside, I knew my commitment to healing and recovery had to be as big as the original damage.

I knew most of the nerve endings for orgasm were concentrated on the clit, but I was accepting that old wounds, trauma and negative emotions could be stored in the walls of my pussy, and more than ever, I wanted that damage to be replaced with healthy tissues and cells. I continued with my breath work sending deep, relaxed breath into my pelvis.

By the time I was ready for another yoni massage, Curtis was on a retreat in Hawaii, so I booked another internal massage with a different male therapist. It had been a few months since the yoni massage with Curtis. This time I felt a tingling when John, the therapist, started massaging inside my pussy. When it felt like too much, I asked him to be still for a minute. I noticed my first instinct was to stop the sensations. I had trained my body to handle years of abuse by disconnecting so I didn't have to feel anything. I didn't realize that choice was also cutting me off from aligning with the deeper part of my being, my essence, my womanness. I wanted to disconnect from the bad, but doing so had also disconnected me from the goodness inside.

"Okay, you can keep going," I said when I was ready. It was becoming a choice of how much of myself I wanted to let back in.

I booked another massage with John a few months later. This time when he touched me, the tears started flowing, not from being scared, but from allowing myself to feel everything. That day when the massage was done, I knew the layers of damage had been replaced with soft, healthy responsive tissue that could feel again. I felt like I was coming home.

# SEVEN
## ORGASMIC MEDITATION

*"Our life is composed greatly from dreams, from the unconscious, and they must be brought into connection with action. They must be woven together."*
—Anais Nin

I became curious about Orgasmic Meditation (OM) after seeing a TED talk online by Nicole Daedone, the founder of OneTaste, an organization dedicated to teaching OM. Prior to discovering Steve Bodansky's work in Extended Massive Orgasm (EMO), I used my body for sex that was hard, fast and disconnected. Sex never felt sensual or intimate. Many times, I closed my eyes to tune out what was happening, even though I may have been with a partner I loved.

OM was a fifteen minute practice focused solely on your partner stroking your clit. There was no intercourse. There was nothing I had to do for the man who was stroking me. OM was a practice that allowed me to become more comfortable receiving.

I signed up for an OM class in Austin on a weekend when I was visiting my daughter, a student at the University of Texas. I noticed that I always took classes in places I visited, never close to home. When I left the courses, I knew I wouldn't see any of the people again. I felt safer revealing myself in the company of strangers.

During an OM, the woman lies in the same position as in EMO, naked from the waist down, as the man (or her partner) strokes her clit for fifteen minutes. After fifteen minutes, the partners share a memory of a moment during the OM, and then close up the OM 'nest' they created for the practice. (A nest is a place for the woman to lie, supported by pillows under her head and knees, as the man sits next to her.) The fifteen minute practice serves as a container wherein the focus of the meditation for both people is the clit. I thought it was weird research, especially working with a stranger, but I recognized that when I'm uncomfortable with something, it might prove to be just what I needed.

The OM class was filled with thirty people, men and women, from their early 20s – the age of my oldest kids – to a woman in her 60s. I was 49 when I took the course. Most of the women were younger than I by a decade or two. There were several men in their 20s, and the rest were 30-50 years old. There were only a handful of people older than I. I felt like one of the matriarchs of the OM room.

Only recently had my age been triggering new insecurities with men. Much of it had to do with my body changing as I went through menopause, even though I still looked much younger than my age. This had definitely been the case the year before, when I went out to dinner in Cape Town, South Africa with a man I'd met through a mutual friend. We were the same age, but I guess he assumed I was younger. We were joined by a friend of his who was in his early 30s. They were both surfers and very charming. During sunset and dinner, they both flirted with me as they filled me in on their adventurous dating life in Cape Town. One rubbed my leg as he told me a story. Then the other moved his chair closer to me so our bodies were touching. If I'd been out alone with either of them, I might have ended up going home with him – whichever one it happened to be – but this night I was enjoying the attention of these two beautiful men. As the drinks flowed, the conversation moved to a story about a woman the older man (who was my age) was thinking about dating until he realized that he "didn't want fifty year-old pussy." They both roared with laughter. I laughed too, not wanting to reveal myself.

Now here I was, sitting in a room for the OM course, and I was the fifty year-old pussy. I decided I would take the course and listen to the lecture but leave before we chose partners for the OM. I imagined being the last one picked, like being in grade school and choosing teams for a kickball game. You never wanted to be the last one.

71

The instructors for the course were Robert, one of the original co-founders of OneTaste, and Jessica, who was at least twenty years younger than I. I took a seat near the end of the second row. It was still close enough to hear the speakers but far enough to be a little invisible. Before class started, the people around me were very chatty. Some of them knew each other from a previous course. I kept to myself and felt safer because both of the seats on either side of me stayed open. I was only there for the course, not to make friends. Just as Robert launched into his introduction, a gorgeous man in his early thirties came in, looked around at the few open seats and came across the room and sat next to me.

"We're going to spend the morning reviewing the principles of OM and orgasm, and then this afternoon you'll have the option to choose someone from this group to OM with," Robert announced. There were nervous giggles throughout the room at the thought of pairing up with a person you just met.

We were asked to say our names and why we were there. The answers ranged from "I want to be a better lover," to many of the women saying "I have trouble having an orgasm". One couple wanted to improve their sex lives, and a young guy admitted, "I don't exactly know where everything is located down there." When it was my turn, I said confidently, "I'm Betsy. I've done other research in Extended Massive Orgasm, and I'm interested in learning how I can expand feeling my orgasm even more. I want to feel comfortable lying back and receiving more."

The cute guy sitting by me went next. He mentioned he was curious about the practice. I made a deal with myself I would stay for the OM if I could OM with Mr. Curious.

In the world of Orgasmic Meditation, orgasm is feeling all the sensations of pleasure, right from the first stroke. Climax is the sensation of going over, getting off, cumming. The goal of most sex is to end in a climax, but most OMs don't. The only goal in OM was for the women to feel each stroke and to see where her orgasm wanted to go, and for the man to find pleasure in the stroking. After fifteen minutes, the partners stop the OM, exchange a favorite moment during the OM and end the practice. No one is ever supposed to go from the OM right into making out or having sex.

During the first break, Mr. Curious asked me if I was taking the communication course the next day.

"No, I'm only signed up for today," I said. "I'm just visiting here. I don't live in Austin."

My mouth went completely dry as I spoke to him. *Please stop talking,* I was thinking to myself, but I went on.

"I have plans with my daughter tomorrow. She goes to UT. She's a junior. But we're not from here. We're from Indiana. But I live in Miami now." *Please shut up*, I thought. I was babbling. I talked a lot when I got nervous with a man. "I've already done lots of research on orgasm," I said, like I was already an expert and didn't really need to be there. I didn't give him a chance to respond. "I'm going to the bathroom." And I got up and walked away.

When I got back from the bathroom, Mr. Curious was at the snack table chatting to a girl in her thirties who looked like Sandra Bullock. *He's looking for his OM partner*, I thought.

I blew my chance.

When we broke at mid-day, the course leaders advised us to have lunch with several people from the class, not to be alone. I went to the bathroom again so I could avoid pairing up for the lunch dates. When I got back, Mr. Curious was walking out the door with the Sandra look-alike and two other attractive women near his age.

I went to get lunch alone, feeling slightly bemused that I was taking the course and slightly uncomfortable that I was a fifty year old woman focused on my orgasm. Maybe I had done enough research. How would I know when it was enough? My twenty-one year old daughter, who knew about the course I was taking, called to see how I was doing.

"It's interesting and educational," I told her. "I wish I had this information when I was your age. We get the chance to OM with someone this afternoon, but I think I'll leave early. It would be weird to OM with someone I don't know." And I was afraid my daughter would judge me if I did.

As I ended the call, I wondered if she wished she had a mom who was researching something else, like cooking or scrapbooking.

I stepped around Mr. Curious as I took my seat for the afternoon session.

"Did you follow the rules and eat lunch with someone?" he asked. How did he know?

"No, I don't like following rules," I said. Mr. C smiled.

"We're going to play communication games to release some of the tension before we move on to setting up the room for the OM," Robert announced. "Let's move all the chairs to the side of the room. Pick some-one and take turns, one at a time, exchanging what you notice about them. Don't be general, like 'you're beautiful'. Describe what you see."

People paired off quickly. I was with a guy who had been sitting in front of me. I went first.

"You have hazel eyes. The outer edges of your eyes are rimmed with brown. You have dimples on both cheeks, but the one on your right cheek is more pronounced when you smile. You have a great smile."

I was also noticing he had something in his teeth from lunch, but I didn't want to say anything about a thing I wouldn't want people to notice. I kept looking.

"Your nose is thin and straight. Your lips are thin, too."

"Switch," announced Robert. "Now the other partner does the noticing. Go!"

He stared at me.

"Your eyes are brown, but the color is faded at the edges."

I watched his eyes trace my face.

"One of your eyebrows is lighter than the other."

He looked closer.

"There is not much hair on that eyebrow."

I wished I had bangs.

I gave him a smile, trying to get him off my eyebrows. Everyone always comments on my great smile.

"You have a few red spots around your forehead."

Asshole. Stop looking so close. I hadn't seen spots on my face this morning.

"They look like pimples, but maybe they're a rash."

I should have spoken up about the food in his teeth.

"Okay. Stop," Robert said. "Find a new partner."

Thank goodness I was done with the noticing.

"This time we are going to practice asking for an OM, but the answer is always No. You need to get used to not having an attachment to getting a Yes or a No."

I looked around for a partner. Everyone was pairing off quickly.

"Everyone has a partner?" asked Robert.

I didn't. It was a clutter of thirty people standing so I couldn't see who was still open.

"Raise your hand if you need a partner."

I raised my hand. I saw the wave of another hand across the room. I walked towards the wave. It was Mr. Curious, and he was the only one in the room I wanted to say yes to.

"Okay, choose who is going first, and for two minutes, you are going to ask the other person to OM. The answer is always No," Robert reminded us.

"Ready, go."

I asked first.

"Do you want to OM?" I smiled.

"No."

Ugh.

"Do you want to OM?"

"No."

I hate this. I want to go back to the noticing game.

"Do you want to OM?" I said.

"No."

Rejection again.

Maybe I could get him to break the rules. I remembered Regena telling me to connect to my pussy when I wanted something.

"Do you want to OM?" I asked again as I thought about my beautiful pussy.

"No." And then he smiled at me.

I thought about the buzz of my orgasm and asked again.

"Do you want to OM?"

He hesitated, smiled again and I swear he nodded a yes.

"No" he said.

"Time." said Robert. "Okay, switch partners."

We switched, and he was just as playful in his asking, and I was just as cheeky in refusing.

We did a few more games, each time switching partners. It was a great way to practice being present with someone and not be attached to the outcome. By the end of the games I'd released my resentment of my first partner noticing my spots. He was only following the rules.

"Okay, we are going to take a break and set up the room for the OM. If you haven't asked anyone to OM, now is the time to find a partner. Or if you don't plan on OMing, then you need to leave the room." I quickly excused myself to go to the bathroom.

One the way to the bathroom, a guy about the age of my oldest son, who was twenty-four, asked me to OM.

"No," I said. He looked disappointed with my response.

"I'd OM with you, but I'm not comfortable OMing with someone your age," I apologized. "I have kids your age."

I remembered I was only supposed to say No.

"Sorry," I said. "No."

I went into the bathroom and decided to stick with my plan to leave. Plus, I knew everyone would be paired up when I returned.

When I walked out, people were starting to set up the OM areas.

I went to get my purse to leave. It was right next to Mr. Curious.

"Do you want to OM?" he said.

"Yes!"

He smiled.

I smiled.

"I'll get my stuff," he said.

Mr. Curious came back with a blanket and three pillows that looked like they were from his couch. He put the blanket down and put a pillow at the end for my head and two near the middle to support my knees.

"So ladies, you can go ahead and undress from the waist down," Robert said casually.

Shit. What have I gotten myself into?

I slipped off my jeans and carefully folded them next to me. I avoided making any eye contact with Mr. Curious.

"Before we start the OM, I want you to face each other, and you'll each get two minutes to say whatever is on your mind. You're not going to have a conversation. You are just going to release any thoughts you have."

I moved to face Mr. Curious. We were both sitting cross-legged with our knees touching. I was naked from the waist down. I was grateful I was wearing a long tunic which kept me covered.

"Ok, first person, start."

I didn't give him a chance to go first. I started talking, fast, the words shooting out of my mouth like a fountain.

"It feels really odd to have someone see my pussy under these conditions. It's also weird that I'll be having an orgasm in a room full of people. I've done other work on orgasm, but I'm super nervous to be doing this in a group. I planned on leaving before the OM because I thought you would ask one of the girls from lunch. I think you are probably closer to my daughter's age then to my age. Why do I feel more comfortable trying this with you than asking the man I've been dating? I also had a man last year make a joke about 50 year-old pussy as being a turn-off, and I turn fifty in a few months. It's hard for me to look you in the eyes. I'm so happy you asked me to OM. Thank you."

He gave me the most empathetic gaze the entire time I spoke. Then it was his turn.

He spoke slowly, cautiously, using half the words I used in the same amount of time.

"Yeah, I think this is weird too…but I'm always open to learning more…exploring more… I like your energy… You are the only person I wanted to OM with today… I'm glad you said yes."

I felt much calmer by the time we both finished speaking our truths.

"Okay, ladies, go ahead and lie down," said Robert. "We have several OM coaches in the room who will come around and guide you through the OM."

I lay back on his blanket. I was grateful he brought something nice. I looked next to me and the guy had brought a blanket that was torn in several places. I felt bad the girl he was paired with had to lie on something that was less than perfect. Her orgasm deserved better.

"Guys, we are coming around and giving you a pair of gloves to use and some lube. If you are working with your wife or partner, you don't need to use the gloves."

I stretched out my legs and crossed them. My tunic covered the tops of my thighs. Mr. Curious was sitting on a yoga block next to me. He draped his left leg over my abdomen. We avoided looking at each other.

"Go ahead and butterfly your legs open," I heard. It was one of the OM coaches.

I opened my legs and the coach helped my partner arrange the pillows under my knees.

My right leg fell open on top of Mr. C's right leg. His right foot gently touched my left foot.

"Start the noticing," said Robert in a tone softer than when he was teaching the class. "Just like we did earlier when we were playing the games. Just notice your partner's pussy and tell her what you see."

I could feel tingling in my pussy the minute Mr. Curious started looking at me.

78

He spoke quietly. "You have a freckle on your upper right thigh. Your outer lips are rose colored and look like flower petals ready to open. Your thighs are flushed red, like you've been in a sauna."

It felt good to be noticed, and it felt compromising to reveal so much of myself to a stranger. A wave of thick heat rolled over my lower body making me think I was going into full menopause at that very moment.

"Thank you," I said.

"I'm setting the timer for fifteen minutes. Guys you need to safe port your partner. Let her know before you touch her."

Mr. C turned and looked at me. "I'm going to touch you now."

"Okay. Thanks," I said, doing my best to make eye contact. I placed both hands on his leg that was draped over me. I liked the circles of connection we had between several different parts of our bodies.

"Once you safe port, start the OM by grounding her. Give a gentle massage to her thighs. Connect to her energy through these first touches."

Mr. C applied pressure to each thigh with the palms of his hands. Rather than rubbing, it felt like he was gently pushing his energy through me. It felt good. It felt safe.

"Tell her you are going to put your hands into position."

One of the coaches showed him how to slide his right hand under my ass. His thumb rested at the bottom of the opening of my vulva.

"Go head and put some lube on your left finger. You are going to rest your left elbow on your left knee. When you're ready to start stroking, let her know you are going to touch her. Always safe port your partner."

Mr. C turned his eyes towards me.

"I'm going to touch you now."

"Okay," I whispered as a surge of water flowed to my eyes. I hoped the tears would wash away the sudden vulnerability I was feeling.

As I felt the soft graze of his finger, I squeezed my eyes shut.

"Start the first stroke at the bottom of her pussy and slowly stroke your finger upward until you reach her clit."

This was the voice of one of the coaches, kneeling next to Mr. C. I hadn't noticed his head between my legs guiding my partner.

I let out a sigh as his finger slid up my pussy. He stopped when he reached my clit.

"Sometimes you have to pull back the hood and look for the clit."

The coach, the voice between my legs was talking again.

"But her clit is already peeking out."

"What's your name?" I heard from between my legs.

My partner looked at me.

"Betsy," I said.

"Okay Betsy," the coach continued. "He's going to focus on stroking the upper left quadrant of your clit. You need to tell him if you want any adjustments."

His stroke was light and airy. Yet although he barely touched me, the sensation was huge. Each stroke left a trail of sparkling energy.

"It feels amazing," I said.

My partner locked in his finger on my clit. Each stroke took me beyond the previous sensation. My high kept going higher. My body stayed completely still, taking in the fullness of the strokes. I didn't want to move a muscle.

I heard the voice between my legs. "Good, Betsy. Do you want an adjustment?"

I breathed deep into my abdomen and felt the next stroke. What did I want now?

"That feels really good," I said. "Can you go even slower?"

The slower touch allowed me to feel even more of my orgasm. It made me think I had felt only about 10% of my orgasm when I chose disconnected, fast, hard sex.

Now I was feeling my orgasm more than ever before with a man I barely knew.

He slowed his stroke down to a micro-movement, and at that point, I couldn't tell where my clit ended and his finger started. Energy buzzed through my pussy like a mushroom cloud, exploding and expanding. Although I wasn't climaxing, I was feeling sensations that were bigger and juicier then I had ever experienced during a climax.

Mr. C continued to stare at my pussy, focusing on each stroke. He reminded me of the lamas I saw at the Buddhist temples in India, sitting in meditation, counting the 108 beads on their malas, one by one, with each prayer.

I silently thanked him for being curious enough to come to class today. I silently thanked him for helping me feel safe. I silently thanked him bringing waves of pleasure through my body.

And then I thanked myself for following my curiosity and my orgasm.

"Two minutes," I heard Robert say.

Without me asking for what I wanted, Mr. C quickened his stroke and took my orgasm to a higher peak. The tears flowed with my orgasm. For years, I only saw value in the end results and now I was feeling the best part of my sex, that place between orgasm and climax where the world melts away, the mind quiets and I was in harmony with the ecstasy of the moment.

"Time," said Robert. "Bring your partner down from the OM by taking a towel, covering her pussy and applying pressure at her pelvic bone. This will help ground her."

I was still high from my orgasm as Mr. C grounded me.

Then he helped me sit up.

I felt immense gratitude for him but wasn't too sure what to say. I immediately moved a few inches away from him, so we weren't touching anymore. I noticed many of the people in the room kept some light contact after the OM. I suddenly realized I had been feeling my orgasm in a room with twelve other couples doing the same thing. I had mostly tuned them out during the OM, and when I did listen, what I heard was a chorus of moans and sighs, the music of orgasm.

I thanked my partner for the OM and left as soon as the class ended. It was weird that we didn't exchange numbers, but in the OM community, your OM partner can be just that, someone to stroke you for fifteen minutes. I walked out of the course and into the hot Texas sun thinking about all the years I hadn't allowed myself to feel pleasure. I wondered how to bring this connection into a relationship with a man that I cared for, so that instead of wanting to move away from him, I'd make the choice to stay and let myself be seen.

Several months later I was back in Texas for an advanced OM workshop led by Nicole. This time I took a seat in the front row.

I hadn't been with any men since the first OM class, but I was interested in taking the advanced class because it covered additional stroking techniques and how to "ask for what you want."

There were several couples in the class. One was a young couple at the beginning of their relationship. Another, had been married twenty five years. Both couples felt stuck in their communication around sex. Nicole asked for a volunteer to demo an OM. My hand shot up. I wanted to pull it down. Nicole pointed to me.

"Okay, get up on the table," she said.

*I don't want to do this,* I thought. I honestly don't know how my hand ended up in the air. Usually I liked to stay hidden.

There was a massage table set up in the front of the classroom. Nicole stood up and patted the table waiting for me. I walked to the table, kicked off my sandals and sat down near the middle. My sundress was long and covered my legs.

"We need a guy to volunteer to be the stroker," Nicole said.

I looked out at the forty people in the room. Several men raised their hands.

Nicole pointed to the guy who had been sitting next to me in the front row. We hadn't spoken the entire morning. I looked at his name tag as he joined me at the table. It said Matt. Nicole handed Matt a pair of latex gloves, and she put a pair on, as well.

"Okay, go ahead and lie down," she said to me.

Matt gave me a shy smile. I could tell he was nervous, too.

I lay back and pulled my dress up to the top of my thighs. I wasn't wearing any panties. I butterflied my legs open.

I didn't recognize the 'me' that was doing all this. It was like I was out of my body, watching myself volunteer to let dozens of people see my pussy. After nearly five years of research, I was finally seeing that in order to change we needed to expose ourselves. When I hid behind my self-hatred, I was not honoring my body. When I hid behind my secrets and shame, I was not honoring my soul. Now, I was listening to a new voice, or maybe remembering what the real me sounded like.

The room was still and silent, like a church sanctuary. Some of the people in the second row were standing to get a better view.

"Go ahead and move closer if you can't see," said Nicole. "I want you to be able to see the nuances of the strokes. I want you to feel her orgasm."

I heard chairs being pulled forward. I looked up – everyone was moving closer. I saw forty sets of eyes, gathered very close to the end of the massage table, all looking at my pussy.

Part of me wanted to run, and part of me remembered that it helped to breathe into the discomfort. So I did. I closed my eyes and tried to tune everyone out. I noticed that didn't feel right anymore, though, so I opened them. I was choosing to stay present and not to disappear. My new voice was constantly overriding the old, wounded one.

Nicole started the OM with grounding, noticing and safe porting me.

My body responded immediately to all the attention on my pussy. I was tingling with energy. I was completely secure in conditions that would have seemed impossible to feel safe in before.


Nicole encouraged Matt to stroke lighter and lighter until he was barely touching my clit. His gentle touch brought about expansive sensation, as if his finger and all the energy around his finger were stroking my desirous clit.

"I want you to say yes to each stroke," Nicole told me.

"Yes…yes…yes…yes…yes…"

Nicole was standing to the left of me, giving verbal adjustments, and Matt was on my right. His right hand cupped my bottom, holding it in place as the index finger of his left hand stroked me. His cheeks were flushed like he was working out. He had beads of sweat on his forehead.

"Relax your neck and shoulders," Nicole said to him.

"Betsy, pull your breath all the way through your body.

"Matt, go even lighter.

"Do you see the changes in the color of her pussy?" Nicole asked the room. "Her labia is swelling and getting darker. So beautiful. And you can see her pussy contracting, but the rest of her body doesn't want to move an inch."

On the inside, sensations were exploding through me. Lines of energy shooting up and down my legs, into my torso and out the top of my head. On the outside, I was looking at Matt and then at Nicole and then to all the eyes looking at me with reverence. It felt holy. I felt holy.

A few months later I was telling my friend Jan about what it felt like to orgasm in front of forty people.

"Weren't you embarrassed to scream in front of everyone?" she asked when I told her about the OM demo.

"I don't scream when I get off," I said. "Isn't that just in porn?"

"My guy doesn't think I get off unless I scream," Jan said. "And when I'm done, I don't want to be touched. My clit is too sensitive."

"I'm the opposite now. My orgasm keeps getting bigger. I can get off for hours," I said. "Even after sex, my body stays turned on. I carry my orgasm with me throughout the day."

She laughed at me, rolling her eyes.

"Why would you want to feel turned on outside the bedroom?" she said. "Aren't you already too busy with kids, work, life?"

I recognized the old me in her response.

"Why wouldn't I?" I answered.

Now that I'd found my orgasm, I wanted to see how I could make the rest of my life feel as good as possible, too.

It meant letting go of the wounds from the past.

# EIGHT
## RELEASING

*"A memory without emotional charge
is called wisdom."*
—Dr. Joe Dispenza

I can't remember if I was taking the photo. I only see that I wasn't in it. And there are five people in the photo, not six.

My youngest son Charlie is about three, and instead of looking at the camera, his eyes are looking down, probably searching for Petoskey stones on the beach. He never wanted to stand still for family photos. Charlie leans into his sister, Lucy, who is four years older than he. Lucy stands in between her brothers and her dad. She squeezes her arms into her chest, not connecting with anyone. Willie must be five years old. He kneels down alone in front, barely in the photo. Sam is eight and is standing in the middle of everyone. I think this was the year his second grade class voted Sam as having the Best Smile. It shows in the photo. My husband stands behind our four children, his arm around Sam. He has a faint smile. Is he smiling at me? Or am I already gone? How could I not want to be a part of this family photo?

Now I remember.

Two weeks earlier, on a sunny day in July, I had given birth to my fifth child, a dead boy I delivered at twenty weeks. He was so small he fit in the palm of my hand. We named him James and then had his tiny body cremated.

Our annual summer vacation to northern Michigan was two weeks later. My husband loaded up the four kids in the Suburban and headed north, leaving me behind. I stayed home in bed, too sad to continue being a mother. I was already finished being a wife.

The person taking the photo was probably our eighteen year-old nanny. She had just graduated from high school.

The first time I posed for a photo in that spot was when my husband took me on vacation when we were first dating. It was eleven years before this photo was taken. We went to stay with his parents at his family's summer beach home on the shores of Lake Michigan. It was the first time I'd met his parents. I had lively dinner conversation and spirited Scrabble games with his father – a lawyer who wasn't above cheating at word games, even when they were against the twenty-six year-old girl who was falling in love with his son.

After dinner with his parents, my soon-to-be husband and I did the dishes while chatting with his mother as she made fresh dough to sit out overnight. In the mornings, we woke to the smell of her homemade sweet rolls.

The following summer, we told his parents we were expecting our first child. His mother wrote down the sweet roll recipe on two handwritten pages and gave it to me at the end of our vacation.

Over the years, we returned to Michigan every summer, first bringing along a newborn, and then toddlers, spending our days playing on the beach and digging through the sand hoping to find a Petoskey stone, a pebble-shaped fossilized coral found only on these beaches. We were told it was good luck to find one. In the evenings, we ate at a ten foot-long cedar picnic table on the porch, with only the stars of the Michigan sky lighting our dinner conversation. And every year at the end of our trip, we would go down to the beach for a family photo.

As we added children to our family, the shoreline started to disappear. The experts thought the water level was dropping due to global warming. Every year, there was less sand and more rocks. It became easier to find Petoskey stones, but less fun to look for them.

In the family photo the summer James died, there was no sand remaining on the beach. It was just my husband and four children left standing on the rocks. It looked like the tide went out and never came back in, but they still posed for the photo, like nothing had changed.

*"We are born of love; Love is our mother."*
—Rumi

The main thing I remember about his birth was the silence. We already knew the baby was dead.

I went for a routine check-up at twenty weeks. I was alone. Through five pregnancies, I'd gone to all my appointments – over fifty of them – alone. Ben never asked to join me, and I never thought to ask.

It was the halfway point for my pregnancy, so I was getting an ultrasound. I was excited to see the body of the new soul in my womb. Becoming a mother had been the best thing that ever happened to me.

I lay back on the paper sheet covering the examination table and watched the nurse put gel on the end of the ultrasound wand. My stomach was tan from a summer swimming with the kids, and it had a hint of a pregnancy curve.

My four other children were at the country club pool with a babysitter, waiting for their Dad and me to join them for dinner. I promised I would bring them the ultrasound photo of their sibling. We all agreed, we wouldn't ask about the baby's gender. I always waited until the delivery to find out. I liked surprises.

The nurse touched the ultrasound wand to my belly just above the tan line of my bikini bottom. My skin was dry from being in the chlorine, and the gel on the wand left a trail as she moved across my abdomen.

"We don't want to know the sex," I reminded her.

"I remember," she smiled. "And it's also written in big letters on your chart."

During my last appointment, a month ago, I listened to the baby's heartbeat for the first time. It was a sublime moment to hear my heart beating along with the baby's heart, two hearts beating in my body at once.

The nurse moved the wand around my belly for several minutes and then held it still. I turned my head away from the ultrasound screen in case anything was revealed. Then she dropped the ultrasound wand.

"I'm getting the doctor," she said without looking back at me. I didn't have time to say anything. She was gone.

My doctor sauntered into the exam room minutes later. He looked like the man in the Marlboro ads. I imagined that if he could, he would dangle a cigarette from his lips as he examined me. He seemed like the type of man who could save the day. He picked up the ultrasound wand but avoided looking at me. He pressed down on my abdomen and studied the screen.

"I've got bad news. There is no heartbeat."

The doctor kept talking, but I had already shut him out.

"Where is Ben?" he said.

"Do you want us to call him?"

"You can let the baby pass naturally or be induced and deliver at the hospital."

I couldn't understand a word he was saying.

When Ben joined me later at the hospital, I was given Pitocin, a drug that induces labor. The delivery room didn't have the activity of a normal birth. It was quieter, and no one was excited. A nurse checked on me on occasion, but mostly I was alone. I could tell my husband was nervous. He kept excusing himself and leaving the room. A few minutes after Ben stepped out of the room to make a phone call, I felt a release at the end of a contraction.

I rang the nurse call button.

"I delivered the baby."

He was so small I was afraid to reach between my legs and pick him up. When the nurse came in, she lifted him to me.

He fit in the palm of my hand.

"It's a boy," she said. Ben stood by my side. The nurse leaned in, put her arms around me and held me as I wept.

The following spring my son Willie, age five, asked me to look at something in the kitchen. "I want to show you what I did," he said in his high squeaky voice.

"Just a minute," I said, thinking that whatever I was doing was more important than what my son wanted me to see.

Willie stood patiently at the hall doorway where we updated the kids' growth by drawing lines on the door frame. It was a rainbow of names, dates and lines that we updated on birthdays or anytime we wanted to remember something special.

"What do you want to show me, Willie?"

He pointed to the door frame. He had drawn a line about twelve inches above the floor and written James next to it. "Do you think James would be about this big by now?" Willie asked.

The next year when we were getting divorced, we sold the house. I tore the growth chart from the door and took it with me. I was never good at releasing things.

My mother never asked me about James. My family doesn't do death and grief well.

I learned to bury my feelings when I buried the dead. The first death in my life was my grandfather. I was eight years old, and it was confusing. I didn't understand what was happening during the service in the church or the cemetery. No one explained death to me, and I didn't know the right questions to ask.

When I became a parent, I finally thought about all the life moments we don't explain to our children. A year after James' death, my husband and I gathered our four young children to tell them we were getting a divorce. The tears flowed from our eyes as the children stood stone-faced. Years later, my daughter told me that after our talk, they went upstairs into one of their bedrooms, and her older brother Sam – only eight at the time – was trying to figure out why we adults were upset. He blurted out, "I don't even know what divorce is."

I held tightly to the grief of losing a baby. I could access my grief in an instant. I couldn't remember how to access my happiness.

*"It's impossible to heal the body without healing the soul."*
—Socrates

I finally learned to grieve ten years after James died when I buried five babies in Africa. I had arrived in Zimbabwe with the dream of adopting an infant. I took six suitcases of baby supplies with me and a blanket embroidered with the name Loveness, the name given to an abandoned baby by the hospital staff a few weeks earlier. She had arrived at the hospital in a dirty wheelbarrow. A local man found Loveness, only a few weeks old, in a nearby field. He loaded her tiny body into his wheelbarrow and pushed her all the way to the hospital. She lived there for nearly a month, dying a few days before I arrived. No one bothered to tell me. I got off the plane thinking I would hold her and ended up burying her instead.

When I went to pick out a casket for Loveness, the head nurse at the hospital said, "There are four more dumped babies in the morgue, can they be buried with her?" Labeling a baby abandoned was horrible; the term 'dumped' was even worse. I couldn't wait to leave.

The only time I saw Loveness was in the morgue. It was on the day she was being buried. I went to see her after she was put into the casket I picked out. The shelves of the morgue were overcrowded with decaying bodies, all unclaimed.

The morgue attendant lifted the lid of the white casket.

Loveness looked peaceful, like she was having a good nap.

She was surrounded by the tiny bodies of the four other dead babies, all boys.

And then a fly landed on her face. I wanted to brush it off, but I was afraid to touch her. It was a hot day, and the air was heavy with the smell and taste of death. I covered my nose and mouth and left.

When I arrived at the burial grounds, the hole was still being dug for the casket. Two men, drenched in sweat from the blazing African sun, used a pick and shovel to dig a hole deep enough for a casket full of babies.

As the casket was lowered into the ground, I was offered a handful of dirt to throw on it. I cringed at having to participate in burying the dead. At the funerals I'd attended, we let the funeral home deal with the dirt. We kept our hands clean.

And then I heard music. Around me the hospital staff who gathered for the burial sang a beautiful song. Even though I was rigid all week from the shock of the loss, the music made my body naturally start to sway. I felt a pulsing in my core, a feeling that wouldn't allow me to bury myself with the babies, a feeling that kept me moving. I danced with the women around me as I cried for the babies.

A few years after burying Loveness, I found the baby box with James's ashes, when I was moving out of the home I shared with my children. It had been fifteen years since I'd delivered him. I gently squeezed the velvet bag with the ashes. They were hard and crunchy. Were they ever soft, like a baby? I didn't remember.

I sat down and prayed to any God that would listen to give me a sign of where to release the ashes.

I was ready.

Within two hours, I got the answer.

An email arrived from my friend Rochelle, inviting me to go with her to Ephesus, Turkey to visit the tomb of mother Mary. While I didn't have strong feelings about Jesus other than acknowledging that he was a fierce but loving man who stood firmly for his beliefs, I did feel a connection to all mothers. I liked the idea of leaving James' ashes at the grave of Mary, the mother of all mothers. At least it felt much better than leaving him in Indiana. I packed the ashes and headed first on a pre-planned trip to

Greece, where I would spend six days at sea on a wooden sailing yacht. This was to be a Qoya spiritual retreat with a group of women, including my mother, who was nearly eighty.

We spent a lot of time on the trip talking about shedding the past.

"What are you ready to let go of?" asked Rochelle Schieck, the founder of Qoya, who was leading the retreat. "What can that energy be alchemized into?"

*Release the ashes in the water*, I wrote in my journal on our last morning on the boat. I'd intended to take the ashes to Ephesus the next day, but I got the strong feeling that I should release them at sea. I had the feeling it needed to be done that day, before we left the boat.

How would I make it meaningful? What words would I say after fifteen years? I got the answers during our final Qoya class.

"When you give yourself permission to feel all of life through your body, even the shadows, even the darkness, even the pain, an interesting thing tends to happen. We don't collapse into our wounds like we might fear; instead we see how strong we are, how courageous we are, and we remember that maybe one day before we were born, we chose this," said Rochelle. "We knew we would come into this complicated creation, and we would stand for love over and over again. Our hearts would break a thousand times, and each time we would understand it was so they could break open. We could embrace our challenges and embrace each other by continuing to come back to love."

Later that day, without telling anyone, I opened the velvet bag. Inside was a plastic bag with the ashes. I looked over at my mother, who was knitting at the back of the boat. Should I say something? I hadn't told anyone about my plans.

I smiled at Mom as I walked past her. Rochelle and three other friends had jumped from the deck of the boat into the water, a twelve foot drop. I planned on jumping in after them. I hesitated at the rail. My friends looked like mermaids laughing and playing in the current. The water sparkled with their joy.

"Jump!" Rochelle shouted to me.

I froze as I gripped the bag.

Suddenly, the small bag of ashes sprang into the water.

"What was that?" said Rochelle.

Mom looked up from her knitting.

I looked to the water scanning for the bag. The ashes had disappeared.

"Just something I was going to let go of in the water," I said.

I had no idea how the bag came out of my hand.

Now he was gone, locked inside plastic.

"It must have been ready to be released," Rochelle yelled as she floated further away from the boat.

Stunned, I walked slowly down the stairs to ease myself into the water. I knew the swim would cover the tears. As I swam towards my friends, something caught my attention off the back of the boat. Changing directions, I dove under the surface and kicked towards the stern. The plastic bag bobbed on the surface, waiting for me.

I opened the bag, and his ashes swirled around me. I lowered my head and slow danced beneath the surface with the ashes of my son.

When we left the boat twenty minutes later to meet our taxi, I sat next to my mother in the small inflatable boat that was transferring us to shore.

"I let go of James' ashes just now," I said quietly to her. "That's what I released on the back of the boat."

Just then our small boat picked up speed and the water sprayed us. My mother reached over and gave my hand a squeeze. It felt like a baptism, a rebirth, a new beginning. It felt like returning to love.

# NINE
## FEELING EVERYTHING

*"To touch the soul of another human being is to walk
on holy ground."*
—Stephen Covey

One of the men I dated during my orgasm research was in a wheelchair, and he showed me that a body can still be whole, even after being broken. I met Martino at a restaurant one night in Miami. During dinner with friends, I noticed a man sitting in the corner, surrounded by three beautiful women. When he smiled, he looked like someone famous, maybe a movie star. He was stunning to look at, but he also exuded a beautiful energy. I could feel him across the restaurant. On my way out of the restaurant, I asked my friend Francesco, the maitre d', if he knew the man. I pointed to the corner.

"Martino?" he said in a loud, thick Italian accent. "*Sì*, you have to meet him." Before I could say yes, I was being whisked in the direction of the table.

"Mio Martino," said Francesco. "This is Betsy. She has four children and no husband."

I rolled my eyes at Francesco. *Thanks for giving too much information.*

Martino and the three women looked up at me as Francesco continued. "And this is Martino's mother and two sisters. They are visiting from Florence. Have you been to Florence? You have to go sometime."

I greeted the women, and as I extended my hand to Martino, I realized he was in a wheelchair. I hadn't noticed.

He shrugged his shoulder to raise his right arm a few inches and then lowered it back to his lap.

95

"Kissing is better," he said. I leaned down and kissed him on one cheek. He smelled really good. I brushed my cheek against his as I pulled away, and then I kissed him on the other cheek.

"Sit down for a drink," he said in very broken English. Francesco had already pulled a chair next to Martino and a glass of champagne was placed in front of me. His mother and sisters all grinned at me. They didn't speak much English. By the time I left an hour later, Martino had made a date for the following night.

His mother and sisters weren't with him that night, only an assistant, Raphael, who drove with him to pick me up. Martino smiled when he saw me walking to the car. I waved and then pulled my arm down quickly when I realized he couldn't wave back. I started to open the door to sit behind him.

"Do you want to walk to the restaurant from here?" I suggested, wanting to ditch Raphael and have Martino to myself.

"He has to help me," Martino said.

"Maybe I can do it," I said. "Just tell me what you need."

Raphael turned off the car.

I stood to the side as he pulled the wheelchair from the trunk and then lifted Martino from the passenger seat to the wheelchair. For one second, as Martino was being placed into the chair, his body was nearly upright and I looked up at him, as I would if he were standing. He was a several inches taller than me. He saw me looking at him and smiled. My heart melted.

"Ok, he's going to park the car near the restaurant in case I need anything," Martino said as he shrugged his shoulder and half-waved his right arm. The fingers on both his hands rolled in, like he was clutching something, except he could never let go.

I started to reach for his hand to hold as we walked and then re-membered. I got behind him, took the handles of the wheelchair and started to push.

Francesco put us at the corner table again in the crowded, popular Italian restaurant. Chairs, tables and people shifted to make room for us to pass by. Two glasses of prosecco were ready for us as we sat down.

"Toast," Marco nodded his head in the direction of the glasses. I picked them both up and clicked them together. "Cheers," I said.

"*Salut*," said Marco. I moved one of the glasses towards him.

"You first," he said. I took a sip and then put the same glass to his mouth and tipped it up and watched as the bubbles rolled onto his lips.

As we talked and ate for several hours, everyone in the restaurant disappeared into the background. I fed him and then me and then him again as he told me about his accident. He had been on a trip to the Maldives with friends ten years earlier, and after a day of swimming and a late afternoon game of soccer on the beach, his friends went in to change for dinner. Martino ran alone into the water and dove, not realizing it was low tide. His neck snapped and he lay on his stomach looking at the bottom of the Indian Ocean, not sure if anyone had seen him go into the water.

"That was ten years ago," he said. "I was twenty-five. Life is different now. That's the past."

His injury left him a quadriplegic.

"I need help doing everything now," he said. "I wish I could hold your hand, but I can't."

During the story, I had reached over and taken his hand, but he hadn't noticed.

"Where can you feel?" I asked.

"Only from the neck up," he said as he puffed some air towards his forehead to blow a few strands of hair that had fallen in his face. I reached over and pushed his hair aside. He closed his eyes for a second as he felt my touch on his face.

"Let's go for a walk," he said.

"Ok." I smiled.

I pushed Martino's chair a few blocks to the beach. I knelt down be-hind him to talk as we both looked at the dark sky full of stars. After a few minutes, I moved to the side of the chair, still kneeling and then to the front. I wanted to talk to him, to be at eye level with him, but I couldn't get comfortable.

"Sit on my lap," he said.

I eased myself on top of him.

"I wish I could hold you," he said. I smiled, wishing that he could hold me, too.

I got off the chair and reached down for a handful of sand. "Tell me when you can feel this," I said.

I took some of the sand and rubbed it on his hand, then his wrist, then his arm and his shoulder. He looked out at the stars and said noth-ing. I moved my hand to his neck and slowly dragged my sand-tipped fin-gers upwards. Nothing, nothing and then he tilted his head back into my hand as I moved closer to his face.

"I feel that," he sighed. "*Grazie mille.*"

Martino and I dated for three weeks before he suggested that he spend the night at my house. He said Raphael could bring him over after dinner and get him ready for bed. If he needed anything, he would tell me what to do. I was nervous, because once he was put in my bed, there would be no one else to help me move him until Raphael returned in the morning. There were so many things we couldn't do, but I loved the idea of talking to him as we fell asleep and waking up next to him in the morn-ing, so I said yes.

It was one of those dates where you literally go straight to bed. If we chose to have dinner or talk before, his assistant would have to be with us, so when Martino arrived, they headed for the bedroom. I went into the kitchen to get a bottle of champagne for us. After ten minutes or so, Raphael came out of the bedroom and told me Martino was ready.

"He's already peed," said Raphael. "If he doesn't drink anything else tonight, he'll be fine until I get here in the morning. If he does need to pee, there is a plastic baggie in the pocket of his jacket. You just put it over his penis. Okay?"

"Okay," I said. "We'll be fine."

He left me his cell number in case I needed him and then he left. I decided to put the unopened bottle of champagne back in the fridge. I stood at my bedroom door, nervous to go in. I wasn't too sure what to expect.

"*Mio Betsy*," he said as I walked in the room.

Martino was slightly propped up on a few of my oversized white pillows. Raphael had changed him into crisp linen pajamas and pulled the duvet so it covered most of his body. His pale teal eyes stood out against his deep tan. I got butterflies as his mouth parted into a huge smile.

"*Mio Martino*," I said. "How did you sneak in here?"

I was wearing a long silk dress, and rather than change into a night-gown, I slipped off my sandals, lifted the covers and climbed into bed next to him. I lay my head down on his chest and listened to the calm beating of his heart as my own heart was racing. His chest hair felt good against my face. His arms were by his side, but I felt his right arm brush against my back as he shrugged his shoulder to try and put it around me. It quickly fell back to the bed.

We stayed like that for a long time, my body pressing into his, hoping that he would feel something even if it was just my soul opening to let him in. I closed my eyes and imagined what it would be like to feel him inside me, to have his hands around my waist, pumping his hips into mine. I thought about him kissing my ass and thighs and licking along the area where my leg and genitals met. I lifted my head to look at him and his eyes were closed, but he had a faint smile on his face, like he was having the same thoughts as me. I unbuttoned the top of his pajamas and moved my hand to caress his chest hair and then rubbed my cheeks and lips along his chest. I was curious to see if he felt anything. I licked his nipple and then looked up at him. Nothing. His tan chest raised and lowered with each breath. I kissed along his collar bone and then up his neck. He turned his head to me just as I reached his face and he brushed his mouth against my lips, then moved his tongue inside me. My body was throbbing with the desire to play with him, to take him in me, to find the places within him that could feel me.

He kissed me and explored my mouth, lips and teeth as if he were probing my whole body. He kissed my cheeks, forehead, eyelids and chin. He kissed anywhere he could reach within his head's range of motion. As he kissed me, I felt a pulse near my thigh, something hard in the bed. I looked down and his cock was sticking up like a tent, propping up his linen pajama bottoms. I looked up to see his reaction. His eyes were closed. I reached down, looped a finger through the waist of his bottoms and tugged. His hard cock popped out. I was stunned.

I looked at him, but he was still motionless, with his eyes closed, waiting for my lips to kiss him again.

"Martino," I whispered. "You're hard."

He pulled his head up a few inches and looked down his body.

"*Fantastico*," he smiled.

"Did you know you could still get hard?" I asked.

"It happens sometimes," he said. "But not much."

I was shocked he withheld this information from me.

"I only get hard for a little bit. Then it goes away. It's not like before."

I guess I assumed that since he was paralyzed from the neck down, it meant that nothing worked.

"Kiss me again," he said. I pulled my dress over my head and climbed on top of him so I could feel his cock rubbing against my clit. I moved my pelvis back and forth and felt his shaft massaging my pussy. He looked at me, but I could tell he felt nothing.

"Am I still hard?" he said.

"Mmm hmm," I said. "You feel so good." I bent forward to kiss him again so he could feel me too. As he sucked my lips and tongue, I felt my pussy flood with juices.

"I want to taste you," he said. I reached down, dipped my finger into my pussy and then brought it to his mouth. He slowly sucked my finger.

"Come on top of me," he said. "I want to have you in my mouth."

I was unsure how to steady myself over him since he couldn't use his hands. I stood over him and then gently lowered myself until my pussy was over his mouth. There was a shock of energy that shot through me when his tongue reached for my clit. I arched my back and dropped my head.

"That feels so amazing," I said.

He continued to kiss, lick and suck me until my legs were shaking from trying to hover over him. As I lifted myself off him, my pussy was buzzing with pleasure, and then I moved my lips back to his so he could feel me again.

"Thank you, my love," he said.

"Thank you, *Mio Martino*," I said.

We both tilted our heads up at the same time to see if his cock was still hard.

It was.

"It's never hard this long since the accident," he said smiling, like he'd just set a world record.

I grabbed another pillow from the bed and put it behind his body so his head was higher. He looked again proudly at his strong hard cock. My mouth was watering wanting to taste him.

I started kissing his neck, in the area he still had feeling, and then worked my way down his chest to his stomach and then to his genitals, hoping that the trail of feeling would follow. I licked along the shaft and circled my lips around the head of his cock. I looked up to catch him gazing at me.

"Can you feel anything?" I asked.

He shook his head back and forth.

"No, but there is a sensation, I don't know where it's coming from. I don't know if my brain is creating it, or if it's something else."

101

I put my attention back on enjoying his cock. I played with his balls and tickled the area from his beneath his testicles to his ass. I *want him to feel me*, I thought.

Suddenly, his legs started gently shaking, and I wondered if something were wrong. I looked up.

"Don't stop," he said. I put my mouth back on his cock, taking just the head of his cock in and out of my mouth for several minutes. He moaned as his legs shook more, and then I felt a stream of warm liquid shooting into my mouth. Our eyes met in surprise.

"Is that my sperm?" he said. I nodded. "That's the first time since my accident."

I pulled myself up and lay my body on top of him, feeling every cell of our bodies melting together. Even though he couldn't lift them from the bed, I could feel his arms around me. If Martino could allow himself to feel everything, maybe I could too.

# TEN
## WHOLE AND HOLY

*"A good orgasm is satisfying, but a great orgasm can be a revelation of your deepest being, unfolding the truth of who you are in ecstatic communion with your lover."*
—David Deida

When the book *Fifty Shades of Grey* came out, I was surprised how many people loved the storyline. Labeled Mommy Porn, the book sold over 100 million copies worldwide. Even Oprah was a fan.

The book was about a sexual relationship between a rich, attractive man in his thirties who introduces a naive young woman into his world of bondage and dominance/submission.

I loved that the book triggered millions of women to explore their bodies and fantasies around sex. But I also saw the potential for more damage if a woman wasn't confident in her sensuality and sexuality. I wondered if women would sink deeper into choosing pain over pleasure, choosing fear over love, choosing to wear a mask and leather and being submissive rather than speaking the truth about what their bodies craved. None of the eight thousand nerve endings in the clit are being honored or pleasured if a woman is tied up, bent over and being smacked with leather.

I was also seeing women and men using porn as a baseline for what sex was supposed to look and sound like. The examples of sex in *Fifty Shades* and in porn are to look outside ourselves for how we wanted our sex to look, instead of listening to our bodies and communicate with our partners so we create the intimacy we want to feel during sex. I know by slowing down and feeling more, I was able to listen to the innate wisdom

103

of my body, and it always showed me which direction I wanted to go next, whether it was with my orgasm, in a Qoya class, or making a life decision.

Around the same time as *Fifty Shades*, a new lover wanted to play harder in bed without asking permission. Maybe he thought all women were turned on by the idea of submissive sex. He didn't ask before he started smacking me on the ass, hard enough to make me recoil in pain. I pulled away and he reached for me again, like it was a game I wanted to play.

"I know you like it," he said, as he continued to spank me harder and harder.

"Not really," I responded as I finally moved away. "It's too much, you're hurting me. What I do like is when you caress my body, like this."

I held his hands over his head so he couldn't touch me and then slid my body slowly down his as I savored the skin to skin sensation. "That's good," he moaned. As different parts of our bodies connected, I noticed different feelings; a tingling, a shiver or a throbbing depending on where we were touching. It was fun research. I explored him first with my body, then my hands, then my mouth.

"Can you do that again?" he said when I kissed along his neck, enjoying the taste and scent of him as I felt him on my lips. His body was covered in goosebumps. My ass was still stinging from his spankings.

As our communication opened, we ended up having really beautiful sex with him treating my body very appreciatively. It wouldn't have happened if I hadn't asked for what I wanted and then invited him to play together in a way that felt good to both of us. We continued as lovers, and on occasion, he would still spank me as a playful way to remind me to speak up for what I wanted. In the end, he told me that my asking for what I wanted was a turn-on, and it reminded him to do the same.

A recent survey revealed that one in every five women in the United States has been sexually assaulted. The UN has reported that one in every three women in the world will be beaten or sexually assaulted. A woman needs to be fully healed from any sexual wounds before she can make a healthy choice to explore bondage, dominance/submission and other forms of sex play. Otherwise, these practices could take her deeper into her pain.

As millions of women and their partners were exploring the sex featured in *Fifty Shades of Grey,* I was moving away from being in bed with toys and distractions and towards choosing sex that was reverent and honored the body, rather than beating it. I was working on slowing down and listening to the song of my orgasm.

When I started treating my body as sacred, I began feeling my orgasm was sacred, too. I stopped making jokes about the classes I was taking. I stopped making jokes about myself.

The more I respected the gift of my orgasm, the more I wanted to bring in a partner who looked at sex as sacred. It also made me consider the energy of the men I was choosing to have in my life. How did they communicate? I found if a man relied on texting, he usually wasn't present in bed because he couldn't communicate, he could only perform. Did they speak with compassion and kindness? What food were they putting in their bodies? How much did they drink or smoke? Even if I was just kissing a man, I was taking in his energy, so it mattered to me how he lived his life and how he spoke of his ex-girlfriends. It mattered if he called to make a date, or text me. It's all connected.

My research had shown me that how we choose to live day-to-day and how we honor our body and orgasm are very similar. After being with many men who had very large cocks and believing that size mattered to both the man and to me, I found the best sex was now with men who communicated and connected before, during and after sex. Size didn't matter when a man knew to pull some of that excess masculine energy from his cock up into his heart and move from that love – the essence we were all born from – during sex, even if we weren't in love.

I wanted to open myself to what some of my female friends on deeper spiritual paths were experiencing with their partners. They were going beyond the orgasm and into a deeper connection to their higher selves, experiencing a spiritual awakening during sex. They were being, as spirituality and sexuality teacher David Deida says, "fucked open to God."

# ELEVEN
## WANDERING AND WONDERING

*"Everything in the universe is within you. Ask all
from yourself."*
—Rumi

The sound of a roar awakened me. It took a few moments to recognize I was not dreaming; I really was sleeping outside on dirt under the dark sky in Africa. I was not in Indiana anymore.

The next roar was even louder. And closer. In a quick leap, I was on my feet, remembering why I was here. Where was Stan, I wondered?

I'd met Stan on a plane six months earlier. I was flying to Africa from the US and met him on the last leg of my flight from Johannesburg to Mozambique. By that point, I had been flying from the US to Africa for over twenty hours and needed sleep. The flight was completely full, and I was the last one to board. When I got to my seat, a man stood up from the seat next to mine to help make room in the overhead bins for all my duty-free shopping bags.

He looked much younger than I. He reminded me of the comedian Chris Rock, if Chris had a head full of dreads. He was dressed in nice jeans, pressed so there was a crease down the leg. He tucked his long legs beneath the seat in front of him. He had on silver Adidas tennis shoes. I was exhausted and ready to sleep during the two hour flight. I closed my eyes. He spoke to me anyway.

"Why are you going to Africa?

"Do you know Portuguese?

"How long will you be there?

"Where do you live in the US?

"Do you like soccer?

"I play professional soccer for a team in Mozambique."

"My name is Stan."

He never shut up, but after a while I didn't mind, because I loved listening to his smooth British accent, courtesy of his prep school education.

By the time we landed, Stan invited me to dinner. I declined.

"My schedule is booked," I said. I was traveling to Africa to do humanitarian work, not to go on dates.

"But it was really nice meeting you," I added.

Six months later, I headed back to Africa. As I changed planes in Johannesburg for the final leg of my flight to Mozambique, I noticed a guy in line a few people in front of me. He was wearing silver Adidas shoes. It was Stan. I decided maybe it was a sign that I was supposed to pay attention to him. We made plans to meet the next day.

Stan picked me up, and we drove several hours through the countryside. He was taking me to meet his grandmother, a shaman based in a rural area. People came from nearby Zimbabwe and as far away as England to see her for healing, protection, and prayer for changes in their lives. She was their connection to the spirit world and their guide for a better life. Her given name was Agnes, but everyone called her GoGo.

At the age of seven, GoGo became very sick, and when she didn't respond to medication, her parents were advised to take her to a sacred area to see a healer. When the healer saw young Agnes, he was told by the spirit world that she possessed the spirit of Shumba, the lion king. To prove her divine connection and to heal her, he told Agnes to go into a cave and find the sacred cloth and staff from the previous lion spirit who had died there. Her parents watched the ailing girl crawl into the dark cave not knowing if she would ever return. Hours later, to the surprise of her parents and local villagers, Agnes walked out of the cave wearing the sacred cloth and carrying the staff of Shumba. She was healed. Now nearly forty years later, our lives crossed after I crawled out of my own version of a dark cave into my life beyond the wounds of my past.

I met GoGo on the evening of a ritual at which she was expected to transform into the spirit of Shumba sometime during the night. Stan told me ahead of time that he'd received permission from GoGo for me to attend. I would be the first white person to witness her in spirit. The rituals were a respected part of the black ancestral history in Mozambique. It was not part of the country's white culture; I was not sure how I would be accepted by the others attending the ritual.

Stan had recently ended his soccer career to return to Mozambique and study with GoGo. During some of the rituals, he worked as her assistant. She was passing down sacred wisdom from the spirits to Stan, a sign that she expected him to continue the spiritual the path he was on.

During the late afternoon drive to the farm under the golden setting sun, Stan and I didn't talk about what I should expect during the ritual. I knew it would last most of the night and into the next day. Part of me didn't want to know too much, because I was afraid I wouldn't go.

We arrived at GoGo's property after dark, and the pre-ritual festivities had already begun. Bright fires burned in two areas. Through the darkness I could see a large, traditional round hut and two smaller structures. There was no electricity. The only light was from the flame of fires, the sparkle of the stars and the glow of the nearly full moon.

When our car arrived at her farm, GoGo greeted me with a warm embrace and whisked me away from Stan. With her hand firmly holding mine as we made our way through the darkness, GoGo led me first to the smaller fire where the women were gathered.

"Kneel down," she whispered to me, "and greet them."

I dropped to my knees, "Ola," I said. Their reserved replies made me wonder what they were thinking as they stared through the fire at my pale skin. I decided we probably all shared the same thought, *What was a white person from Indiana doing at a sacred ritual in Mozambique?*

GoGo took my hand and guided me across the property to the bigger fire where all the men were sitting on tree stumps and homemade benches. Behind the men, hanging from a tree, were two animals skins stretched across the branches. It was too dark to see what kind of animals they had been. The skins weren't big enough to be from cows. In the dark, the hanging skins looked like something you would see in a horror film. I wondered what the rest of the animal was being used for.

The men's group chatted animatedly in Portuguese, Mozambique's official language. They grew quiet as GoGo and I approached. Once again, I knelt down.

"Ola" I said, this time very softly, my vocal cords feeling strangled by my nerves.

No one responded. GoGo put her hand on my shoulder; her touch calmed the butterflies in my stomach.

"Greet them again, louder this time," she said.

"Ola," I said as I made eye contact with twenty curious pairs of eyes around the fire.

"Ola," they all responded. Through the dark, I could see the whiteness of their teeth as they smiled.

GoGo's introduction seemed to be the only blessing I needed to be accepted into the pre-ritual preparations. I scanned the group for Stan, but he wasn't there. I wished I could ask him what would happen next.

After our formal greetings, I followed GoGo into the largest hut, a round structure with solid mud walls and a straw roof, typical of Mozambican villages. Every bit of wall space was lined with piles of food, blankets and supplies to sustain the tobacco farm run by GoGo and her husband, Sekuru. There was a small fire pit in the middle of the room. GoGo sat on one side of it and motioned for me to sit across from her, where an older woman was already seated on a straw mat on the cold, hard cement floor. The old woman patted the floor next to her. I sat down.

"This woman made all the beer for the ritual tonight." GoGo said to me. "It's an honor to be asked to do so."

I looked at the older women and made a gesture of thanks to her. She reached over, touched my long brown hair and laughed. She was well into her 70s, and it was the first time she'd been near a white person.

I stared across the fire at GoGo as she spoke to the older woman in Portuguese. I couldn't follow what they were saying. Every so often, GoGo poured black powder from a hollow gourd into her left hand. She didn't offer any to me. With her right hand, she took a pinch of the powder and inhaled it.

The powder was called snuff; the locals also called it black cocaine. It's considered an offering, allowing her to connect to the spirits. The snuff is ground from the leaves of a tobacco plant grown in only one area of Zimbabwe, just over the border from Mozambique. It's grown by a few elderly women who are entitled to handle the sacred plant. Everything around a spirit ritual has a purpose and is considered sacred, including the planting and harvesting of the snuff.

I kept my attention on GoGo, hoping to see how she went into spirit. Other than an occasional break to take more snuff, Gogo stayed in conversation with the women who were passing in and out of the hut. This went on for hours. As I often did during trips to African countries, I sat and waited.

Outside the hut, I could hear singing and music. I excused myself and walked outside. I was hoping to find Stan – once again, I wanted to ask him what would happen next. The air was thick with the energy and desires of people drinking, dancing and waiting for answers. I saw about forty people, all moving their bodies to the beat of drums and the *mdiba*, a piano-like instrument made from a gourd. Homemade beer was being passed around as well as the sacred snuff.

I saw Stan in the crowd. He looked more African that night than he did on the plane when I met him. On the plane, he spoke only about being a pro soccer player. Seeing him dancing barefoot under the full moon made me think he was more comfortable here than on the soccer field. When he saw me, he waved and walked away from the group. He explained that during rituals, women and men stay mostly separate. Only virgins, the elderly, or women who have abstained from sex for a long time are allowed to prepare the food. Sex is prohibited for everyone during the days and nights of the rituals.

I looked at Stan as he spoke and suddenly felt very attracted to him. Seeing a man revealing his true self in his most authentic environment was a turn-on. If this had been a regular party, I would have flirted with him, even though he was fifteen years younger than I. He walked with me to the smaller fire, where the women were gathered.

He told me that some of the people were from the local village, but many had come from much farther away. Most didn't have cars, and either walked or took a two hour ride on crowded public transport for five dollars, a huge price to pay in a country where the average monthly salary is eighty dollars. The people all came seeking the same thing: advice and guidance from the spirits of their ancestors and animal spirits channeled through GoGo. It was not unlike my journey going to classes and working with sex experts to find my orgasm. Everyone was searching for something.

Stan left me with the women. The moon was high in the sky, but I had no idea what time it was. As the temperature dropped, I started to shiver, so I moved closer to the fire. I had leggings under my cotton dress but like everyone else, my feet were bare.

A young girl appeared with a heavy blanket for me. The older woman who made the beer came out of GoGo's hut and joined me at the fire. For warmth, she sat next to me so our bodies were touching, our bare feet inches from the fire. We covered ourselves with the blanket.

Even without beer or snuff in my body, I began to feel high with anticipation, like I did when I was in my orgasm.

During rituals, the beer, dancing, drums and snuff are all offerings to the spirits. The spirits like a good party! As the music grew louder, we were called to dance.

The men were in the center, closer to the musicians. Everyone's bodies pulsed to the beat of the music. The women let out loud ululations, a primordial sound to let the spirits know we were calling them in. I danced on my own among them.

I caught a glimpse of Stan dancing among the men. We made no exchange of smiles, just eye contact. I wished I could dance next to him, feeling his arms around me to keep me warm. I wanted to feel his hips melt into mine as we moved to the music.

Minutes later, one of the women handed me a fleece jacket.

"Stan sent this for you. He doesn't want you to be cold," the woman said.

After an hour or so of dancing, we were asked to follow GoGo down a dirt path to a sacred tree. Clouds had moved in and were blocking the light of the moon, so it was hard to see even a few feet in front of me. I was thankful when a woman grabbed my hand to show me the way.

GoGo knelt before the tree with the man who had requested the ritual to change his luck after a series of bad events in his life. His marriage was struggling. He lost his job. After several months of healing and readings with GoGo, she recommended the ritual to align the man with the spirits of his ancestors and to provide healing for his path forward.

I felt fortunate to witness such a sacred part of the culture. I also felt scared standing in the middle of a dark field in an area that was home to lions and other wildlife. I was the only white person present, and it did cross my mind the spirits could call me in to be sacrificed, like the animals whose skins hung on the tree. No one knew where I was. Maybe I should have researched this further before I said yes.

As we gathered around the sacred tree, I felt an energy moving closer to me. I looked behind me. It was Stan. I felt safer with him nearby.

Three gourds of homemade beer had been left at the tree earlier in the day as an offering to the spirits. GoGo instructed the men to pass the beer. We were each to take a drink. As I was handed the first gourd by an older man who looked frail and had been coughing a lot, I tried to remember what diseases one catches from shared drinking vessels. I took a sip out of respect for the ritual and then passed it on. As I drank from the third gourd, the smell of the beer was so strong that I felt like I would vomit if I tasted it. I tipped the gourd, let the liquid wet my mouth, and then passed it to the next person.

When the ritual at the sacred tree was complete, the group wandered back to the fires near the huts and continued dancing, singing and calling in the spirits. I made my way to the women's fire. The dirt on the ground was cool from the evening air. I wished I had socks. I curled up on a straw mat next to the fire and pulled my body into a tight ball, trying to stay warm. I was cold and uncomfortable and wished I could be in a bed.

The roar of a lion woke me. The sound was terrifying. My heart pounded rapidly as I jumped to my feet, terrified that the animal was ready to attack. The roar came again. I saw a figure lunging towards the larger fire. It was GoGo, but it wasn't GoGo. Her body was hunched over and a long black cape hung around her shoulders. She carried a long, thick black stick, a little smaller than a cane. It must have been the staff Stan told me about – the one she found in the cave when she was young.

She let out another roar as she joined the dancing by the fire.

I walked closer, trying to make eye contact, wondering if I could still see GoGo in her eyes. But what stared back at me were the dark intense eyes of a lion, the eyes of Shumba. I backed away.

Everyone continued dancing until Shumba knelt down near the fire. She spoke in Shona, the indigenous language of nearby Zimbabwe. Stan sat next to me to interpret. Shumba offered advice from the ancestors to the man who was holding the ritual. She then went around the circle and gave readings and healing to anyone who asked. I kept my eyes on her, curious to figure out how her features had changed from those of the woman I'd been sitting with earlier to the features of a lion. The skin around her mouth and nose was lighter. Her back was slightly hunched, and her feet and hands met on the ground, like paws. When GoGo greeted me on my arrival, her energy was light and welcoming, but now as Shumba, her energy was intimidating and powerful. Shumba looked at me and stopped. Her voice got louder. She sounded angry. I followed Stan's lead and leaned my body forward, bowing in the direction of Shumba while softly clapping my hands to show gratitude. Stan started interpreting Shumba's words.

"You all judge this white woman because of her color. She has not come here to colonize our country. She has come here to help the children. She has a bigger heart than any of you."

Shumba shook her staff as she spoke and then pointed it towards me.

"Shumba wants you to take her staff," Stan whispered.

I reached out and grasped one end. For a moment, Shumba held the other end, and we looked deep into each other's eyes. She released her end and continued talking.

"You are to stand with the staff and speak your desires to the four corners of the world," said Stan. "You need to say your desires in every direction, raising the staff towards the sky as you speak."

I stood, raised the stick and felt all the eyes on me. As I started to speak, Shumba turned her attention to the next person.

"Keep going," Stan whispered to me. "Say everything you want in life, all your dreams. When you're done, pass the stick back to Shumba."

As I lifted the staff high and started speaking my desires, everyone disappeared into the background. My words were directed to the moon and the stars.

"I desire healing for my family. I desire radical forgiveness for myself and others. I desire protection and opportunity for the children in Mozambique. I desire my projects to be supported. I desire to share the stories of the marginalized voices of society. I desire to find love again with a man who thinks with his heart. I desire to always remember that the energy that created the world is in me."

As I spoke, as I raised the staff and moved slowly in the four directions. It felt like the whole world was listening. When I was done, I knelt down near Shumba and passed the staff back to her. She took it, lifted it to the skies and roared more words.

Stan leaned over, "Shumba told the spirits of the ancestors to honor your dreams."

All around me, women clucked their tongues, ululating, and men shouted in their approval. I bent low and clapped my hands in gratitude and whispered "Thank you."

*"The mystical life is at the centre of all that I do and all that I think and all that I write."*
—W.B. Yeats

The ceremony lasted several hours. When I made my way back to the smaller fire to sleep, someone covered me with several wool blankets. The next morning, the ground that had been so cool during the night was already warm from the blazing sun.

Stan and I left later that day to drive back to the bed and breakfast where I was staying. It was past sunset when we arrived. I had to be up early the next morning to drive to a different part of Mozambique, but I wasn't ready for our time to be over. I was still trying to digest the all-night ritual with Shumba and figure out how it all fit into my life. I invited Stan to join me for a glass of wine on my patio.

As we shared wine under the darkness of the sky, I noticed all the stars, more than I had ever seen. I watched Stan's full lips as he told me about his father leaving his mother when he was two. He spoke of his mother's sacrifices to get him a better education. She made sure he went to the best prep schools in Mozambique on a soccer scholarship. His mother took buses all over the country to watch his games, even if the time and expense meant sacrificing in other areas of her life.

We were sitting a few feet from each other, but our energy felt intertwined. His description of his life penetrated my soul, like his spirit was talking to my spirit. We weren't trying to impress each other or seduce each other. We were engaged beyond our colors, our ages and our countries.

The electricity was off for the night, so when we moved into the bedroom, we undressed each other by candlelight. Naked, we stood holding each other, breathing together, aligning our inhalation and exhalation. I felt his engorged cock between my legs, but there was no rush. My lips melted into his when he kissed me. The kiss sent a spark through my body. I arched my back and pressed my hips into his. He leaned down and took one of my breasts into his mouth, rolling the nipple with his tongue while he caressed the other breast with his hand. I arched further and felt my heart open, like a flower ready to bloom. We moved together to the bed, our bodies in sync, as if a magnetic energy was keeping us together.

He looked into my eyes as he softly stroked my clit and then gently pulled the out lips of my pussy open. I started to reach for his cock, but

he moved my hand back to the bed, his gesture coaxing me to only receive. I relaxed and spread my legs further apart. My body was perfectly
still, but every part of me was lit up with the vibrant currents of a storm
brewing. A zing of energy shot up my spine and out the crown of my
head as his soft touch pulled my orgasm out of me until it felt like I was
floating above my body. He kept me there for a long time, stroking my clit
and lightly rubbing just inside my pussy, so that I stayed on the verge of
climax without going over. I was in a zone where everything was flowing
to me and from me. I wasn't rushing towards the climax. I was savoring
feeling the present moment, accepting my orgasm as was, accepting my
life as was, without any attachment to what came next.

This time, when I reached for him, he allowed me to stroke along his
strong shaft and over the glistening head of his cock. Our movements
were slow, matching our breath. We were touching each other with the
lightest strokes and staying connected with our eyes. He finally disconnected for a moment to put on a condom, and then he lowered himself
so his cock rested at the entrance of my vulva. He smiled when my pussy
pulled him in and I smiled as I noticed I was feeling everything, everywhere. I felt the tingle in my clit and the walls of my pussy dripped with
ecstasy as my head, heart and spirit filled with peace and pleasure. I remembered we were here to love. I remembered God was love.

I was surprised to find God in my orgasm.

# TWELVE
## HEALING THE WOMB

*"I believe in God, only I spell it Nature."*
—Frank Lloyd Wright

The year I turned fifty, I took a trip to Delphi, Greece. According to Greek mythology, Delphi was considered the origin of the world, the place where man was closest to God. I joined a group tour of the ruins of the temple built to honor the god Apollo. Early Greeks came to the temple to ask the oracles, or fortune tellers, about their futures.

"The oracles were always young girls of fourteen or fifteen," said our gregarious Greek guide. "People would come from far away to ask them questions. A priest would be nearby, allowing the people in one by one. But after a while there started to be a big problem, because the oracles were so young and beautiful that the priests started sleeping with them, and this was causing lots of trouble."

She paused, and I looked out at the ruins, trying to connect my history to this ancient, sacred site, a place where heaven and earth met.

"So they solved the problem by replacing the young oracles with fifty year-old women so there wouldn't be the temptation to sleep with them."

The end of my orgasm research for this book coincided with my body going through menopause. I was in my early fifties. My body was changing. I was carrying more weight in my stomach and hips. I liked the new curves, but several men made negative comments based upon how they thought I should look. I didn't allow their comments to sting me like the opinion my sister shared about my body when I was sixteen. I finally realized that someone probably said the same thing to her and she believed it. Maybe she believed she was less worthy of a man's attention if her body carried extra weight. I chose not to believe it. I'd been taught and trained to hate the woman in me and I was done holding onto that message. I found myself falling even more in love with my body and wondering at the extent to which we live in a society that only sees the exterior – can't they feel the goodness in my soul? Can they feel the goodness in their own souls? There is no room for self-hatred and self-loathing. We are born with our body, mind and soul, and each should be deeply honored and appreciated.

I used Dr. Christiane Northrup's book *The Wisdom of Menopause* as my bible and I used my own innate wisdom to make the best choices for myself. Many friends were taking hormones, both orally and through injections, to alleviate some of the bothersome menopause symptoms like heat flashes, low energy, poor sleeping, weight gain and moodiness. A few friends relieved their symptoms by having hysterectomies to remove their wombs. While I did experience more highs and lows, I also honored the imbalance. I was grateful to feel everything, especially after years of not feeling anything. I let myself cry when I was sad, I rested when I was tired, and I tried to take longer walks to make up for the unexpected weight gain. I listened to my body to hear what she needed. And unlike the oracles in ancient Greece, I was also enjoying sex more than ever.

The summer I finished this book, I was invited to Peru, a place that didn't make sense for me to go to, but I trusted feeling the yes in my body when the invitation came to join my friend Rochelle on a Qoya retreat to work with shaman in the Amazon. I thought I was going to experience the beauty and power of the Amazon, but like many people and places I was pulled to, the trip ended up meaning so much more. It was a last piece of the puzzle that I didn't know was missing.

Before the trip, a friend told me that Peru works on the higher chakras of the body. It was a chance to open my heart, to feel safe in speaking my truth and tuning into the wisdom of my third eye, the connection to higher consciousness. It had been over ten years since my near death experience. I always wondered why the voices had said I was supposed to come back – what was I meant to do? Maybe I would find the answer in Peru. Maybe I'd already found it.

*"I feel there is something unexplored about woman*
*that only a woman can explore."*
—Georgia O'Keeffe

By the time I arrived in Peru, it had been several months since I'd had a period. Now that I was menopausal, I always wondered which period would be my last. For so many years, I'd felt shame around my pussy and periods. During my healing and research, I learned to honor my monthly bleeding as a sacred time for my womb, but sometimes it felt like I'd got the message too late. I spent too many years disconnected from my essence, from the gift of being born a woman.

One of the guides for the trip was a shaman from Chile, Marcela Lobos. Marcela and her husband, Alberto Villoldo, lead shamanic spiritual retreats to sacred spots around the world, connecting people to the ancient wisdom of the plants and the spirit energy. Earlier in the year, Marcela had been meditating in the jungle and was told "to heal the lineage of the womb."

"The womb is not a place to store shame and grief," she heard in the jungle. "The womb is a place to create and give life."

When Marcela shared her vision to heal the lineage of the womb with us, I felt a twinge in my lower body. I'd been so focused on healing my pussy and feeling my orgasm, I never considered the importance of my womb, a place that held babies and dreams. That night when I went to bed, I placed both hands over my womb and said, "The womb is not a place to store shame and grief. The womb is a place to create and give life."

When I woke up the next morning, I felt a warm liquid between my legs. I reached down and saw bright red blood on my fingers. My period! I remembered being so scared and ashamed when I got my first period. Now I was grateful to have one more chance to honor my bleeding and my womb. I was happy to feel every juicy part of being a woman. It was reclamation of my womb and my legacy as a woman.

It was one more chance to celebrate myself.

As always, my response was "thank you."

# THIRTEEN
## COMING HOME

*"Love sometimes wants to do us a great favor: hold us
upside down and shake the nonsense out."*
—Hafiz

My travel took me all over the world – some of it for work, much of it
alone – but I always saved Venice to see someday with a man. It seemed
too romantic a place to go by myself. Or maybe I didn't want to give up
on the fairy tale of being whisked off and serenaded in a gondola with my
Beloved. Finally, at the age of forty-nine and hearing that the city may
eventually be submerged, I decided to give myself the gift of a few days in
Venice, minus the groom. Venice was sinking, and it felt like I was running
out of time for the fairy tale.

I ended up there as part of a cruise I was taking alone. With my
fiftieth birthday approaching in a few months, I felt the need to do more,
see more, feel more.

I'd have three days to explore Venice while the ship was in port. The
previous ten days of the cruise had been to some of the most exotic and
spiritual cities – Istanbul, Ephesus, Athens, Mykonos, Sardinia, Rhodes
and Corfu. Every day had been a chance to explore and to discover the
rich histories of cities whose landmarks are now tourist attractions. People
used to go to many of these places to pray. Now they go to buy souvenirs.

The morning our ship pulled into the canal, I was on my daily run
around the deck. When I first saw the islands of Venice rising up from the
water's edge, tears came to my eyes. I was not sad for the person who
never made it to Venice on her fairy tale honeymoon. I was crying because I gave myself the gift of Venice, anyway.

With Venice off the starboard side, I continued my run around the deck. I could feel the strength in my quads and the stretch in my calves with each step. I pulled my stomach muscles tighter, still aware of the curve of my belly. Behind the curve was a womb that had given birth five times. Behind the curve was my history – all the joys and all the pain. Behind the curve was the strength of my body, running towards the present moment, trying to catch up after being so caught up in my past. Looking off the port side, I watched the boats on the canal. Several Italian men smiled and waved to me. I felt like the universe was giving me a wink and saying "You are not alone in Venice. Go enjoy your honeymoon."

*"Don't let the past, remind us of what we are not now."*
—Crosby, Stills, Nash & Young

As I was finishing this book, I unexpectedly ended up back in Indianapolis, the place I'd been running from my whole life. My grown children were home for the summer, and we met for family dinners when everyone was available. At other times I enjoyed quieter meals with just one or two of my children. I also shared meals and meaningful conversation with a few close friends in Indiana.

My pace was slow for a change. For the first time, I was not trying to leave Indiana and the past. I noticed more, observing that a hydrangea plant I'd planted years before at my former home was now blooming in the shape of hearts.

Most mornings, I woke up early to watch the sun rise over the lake, something I never did when I lived there. I would make a cup of tea and sit on my dock, taking in the exquisite colors as the sky changed from gray or dark blue to pink and orange. Every morning, I savored sitting with the darkness as it turned to light.

To break up my writing days, I walked a favorite path along the White River canal. The path led to the Indianapolis Museum of Art where the first iconic LOVE sculpture by artist Robert Indiana was installed in 1970 when I was seven. The sculpture, worn from years of structural damage, had recently undergone repairs to return the color to its original appearance. I used to run on the dirt path when I was a teenager. Now, the path was well groomed and connected into 100 acres of trails around the art museum. My walk took me near the street of my childhood home where I was molested when I was six, and my piano teacher's home where I was accosted by the boys. The path went by the parking lot where a guy in high school forced himself on me. I walked it every morning on this trip, discovering new trails and making new memories.

A local man asked me out on a date, and I reluctantly agreed, even though I didn't want any more ties to Indiana. *Just one date*, I thought.

We met for dinner at a gourmet restaurant in a nearby farm community. We talked and laughed for several hours despite not agreeing on much. He was handsome, interesting and engaging. I was surprised how much I liked him.

After dinner, he took my hand and walked me across the one-lane street and through a small field surrounded by mature oak trees. The grass was vibrant green and alive with the moisture from a summer rain earlier that day. The smell reminded me how much I used to love lying in the grass when I was younger, my body connected to the earth as my mind connected to the sky.

I started talking more, which I did when I was nervous. I started to ask him to tell me something most people didn't know about him. He leaned in and kissed me mid-sentence. It had been a long time since I'd kissed someone in Indiana.

As his lips brushed my mouth, I felt a wave of joy in my pussy. He slowly unbuttoned my jeans and gently moved a hand down my stomach, reaching for my clit. *Too fast*, I thought for a second. I took a breath and listened to my body. I wanted to keep kissing him and to feel his fingers on my pussy. I let him continue.

I remembered a recent conversation with a friend who said that you should never sleep with a man on the first date if you wanted to get a

124

commitment from him later. She'd read it in a book. And then I remembered I wasn't looking for a commitment; I wanted to enjoy my body and to feel pleasure. I wasn't stuck in the past or thinking about the future. I wiggled out of my jeans, and he laid me down on the green grass.

I checked in with what I desired and knew I wasn't ready to have him inside me, especially without a condom and a more detailed conversation about sex. He took off his pants, revealing a beautiful cock, and then he lay in the grass too, undressed from the waist down. He worked his mouth from my lips to my breasts, to my belly and hips, as his fingers lightly stroked my clit. I felt the orgasm instantly.

I kept my eyes open and took in the scene around me, amused that was enjoying myself back home again, in Indiana. The fireflies were just starting to light up as the butterscotch sun faded into the nearby cornfields. I looked at the clouds and played my game, trying to break them up as I focused on feeling everything. I felt the wetness of the fresh grass on my lower back and ass. And then I felt the caress of his lips on my pussy. Sublime.

I had been all over the world healing and searching for an orgasm that felt holy and sacred. Now in Indiana, for the first time, I was feeling all eight thousand nerve endings because I felt holy and sacred. I looked up at the cloud just as my mind made it disappear, and I silently said, Thank you.

# EPILOGUE

Two days after that memorable first date, I started to feel itching on my back and butt. Poison ivy. I checked in with my date, and he had it all over his legs and genitals where he had been lying in the grass.

A week later, after the poison ivy cleared, we went on a second date. The research continues.

# ACKNOWLEDGEMENTS

Thank you to my children for the privilege of being your mother, especially to my daughter Lucy who inspired me to become a better woman so she would have a better role model. And, yes, your orgasm matters as much as your brain.

Thank you to my mother for showing me how to go love again, even after loss.

Thank you Tara Dixon for listening and holding near daily sacred space as I researched and wrote. Depending on what I needed, you showed up as a friend, a sister, a mother and a midwife as I gave birth to each chapter. I am grateful.

Thank you Dee for a friendship that spans a few divorces and many more decades. Thank you for living so many of these stories with me.

Thank you Julie for always cheering me on.

Thank you Jeanne Louise Mayhue for 'seeing' me.

Thank you Rochelle Schieck for creating Qoya and dancing with me on in five continents (so far).

Thank you Melissa Zimmer Pierce, Nancy O'Malley and Paul David for being extra antennas for me when I forgot to trust myself.

Thank you Ann Moller for your divine insight.

Thank you Joyce Maynard and the 2013 and 2014 Write-By-The-Lake writers who encouraged me to tell this story.

Thank you to my Miami writer's group – Andrea, Christina, Jeanne, Melanie, Nick and Jeffrey.

Thank you Dan Wakefield for inspiring me as a filmmaker and writer.

Thank you Ingrid Sato for listening patiently to my stories before I was ready to reveal myself.

Thank you Janet Galipo and Laura Day, two leaders in their fields, for teaching me to work with my own innate wisdom to heal.

Thank you to some of the "experts": Regena Thomashauer, Steve and Vera Bodansky, Nicole Daedone, Robert Kandell and Dr. Anne Davin.

Thank you to my boy friends, lovers and ex-husbands for loving me during the time of life when I wasn't loving myself.

Thank you to my tribe of 'sisters' who inspire me with their lives: Fiona Woods, Susie Sourwine, Camille Sabbey, Becca Kannapell, Linda Kannapell, Nicole Grosman, Danielle Finnegan, Stacy Phillippe Rauch, Kris Simpson, Jen Foxworthy, Amy Smith, Lauren Smith, Karen Quinones, Patricia Costa, Melanie Erickson, Lisa Trudeau, Dr. Deb Kern and Mindy Goldstein; and, to my birth sisters, Sharon and Susan; and, to my god sisters, Wendy & Cathy.

Thank you Mark Shaw for always reminding me a miracle may just be around the corner.

# RESOURCES

**Qoya**: Qoya is a workout for the body mind and soul that liberated my spirit, connected me to radical self-love, tuned me into my inner wisdom and reminded me that even in the most challenging times, dancing is always an option. To learn more about Qoya and the founder, Rochelle Schieck, go to www.loveqoya.com.

**Dr. Christiane Northrup**: A pioneer in women's health and wellness. Every woman should have her book *Women's Health, Women's Wisdom* on their bedside table.
www.drnorthrup.com

**Tosha Silver**: Tosha's book *Outrageous Openness* is a soulful and playful blueprint for living your soul's purpose (and usually it's much better than what your ego has planned for you). Find her books and meditations at www.toshasilver.com

**Laura Day**: Laura is a gifted intuitive and healer. Her workshops were valuable for me as I learned to trust my own insight.
www.practicalintuition.com

**Janet Galipo**: Janet Galipo is a BodyTalk practitioner based in Miami Beach. Thank you Janet for healing my voice, inspiring me to become a BodyTalk practitioner and saving my life when I went into anaphylactic shock.
www.janetgalipo.com

**Regena Thomashauer "Mama Gena"**: Regena is author of several books and the head of the School in Womanly Arts based in New York City.
www.mamagena.com

**Kitty Cavalier**: Kitty teaches courses in burlesque and seduction. You can find more info and her book *Sacred Seduction* at www.kittycavalier.com.

**Melanie Erickson**:  Melanie is an exceptional healer and soul whisperer.
www.soulplay.us

**Joyce Maynard**: Joyce teaches writing courses in the US and at her home
in Guatemala.
www.joycemaynard.com

**Dan Wakefield**: You can find info on Dan's books (including *The Story of Your
Life: Writing Your Spiritual Autobiography*) and courses at www.wakespace.com.

**OneTaste**: I highly recommend Nicole Daedone's book *Slow Sex*.

For more information on orgasmic meditation: www.onetaste.com

**Steve Bodansky**: Reading Steve's book *Instant Orgasm* is a great first step in
honoring your orgasm.
www.extendedmassiveorgasm.com

**Sheri Winston**: Founder of The Center for the Intimate Arts. Author of
*Women's Anatomy of Arousal* and other books.

**Gaia Budhai**: Gaia teaches an amazing course in Transformational Breathing.
The course is not designed for orgasm, but after I worked with Gaia, I was surprised how the breath work led to more expansion in my orgasm.
www.gaialivingarts.com

**S Factor**: Sheila Kelley and staff teach soulful courses in pole dancing.
www.sfactor.com

**Debbie Rosas, Founder of NIA:** Debbie reminds us to enjoy our bodies, move
our hips and celebrate being a woman.
www.nianow.com